Manual of Non-formal Education

Attention Authors

'We Convert Fighters into Writers.' That's the motto of Manas Publications since more than four decades. Our message to the world is that India can win the battle not only by the bullet but also by the pen. There is no dearth of intellectuals in our country, but their knowledge is confined to them only. No sincere effort has been made by any other publisher to channelise their knowledge in national interest. That is why the talent of a large number of intellectuals remains latent. An author transforms his knowledge into a manuscript, and it is our job to spread his/her knowledge by converting it into a beautiful book. For over four decades, Manas has been motivating the intellectuals by publishing their manuscripts and would like to publish your manuscript too. So if you or your colleagues have any manuscript ready for publication or are working on it, kindly contact us with detailed synopsis and list of contents. We will transform your work into a valuable publication. If you wish, we can also suggest you the suitable subjects for writing the books related to your area of expertise. Manas is known for its publishing quality and commitments. We take utmost care in production and give wide publicity to the book as well as its author through our national and international distribution network.

Manual of Non-formal Education

Peace Corps
Center for Field Assistance &
Applied Research, USA

Manas Publications
(We Convert Fighters into Writers)
New Delhi-110002 (INDIA)

MANAS PUBLICATIONS
(We Convert Fighters into Writers)
(Publishers, Library Suppliers, Importers & Exporters)
4402/5-A, Ansari Road (Opp. HDFC Bank)
Darya Ganj, New Delhi-110 002 (India)
Off. ✆ 23260783, 23265523, Fax: 011-23272766
E-mail: manaspublications@vsnl.com
manaspublications@gmail.com

ISBN 978-81-7049-440-9
₹ 295/-

Designed at
Manas Publications

Printed in India at
Harmain Offsets, Delhi
and published by Mrs Suman Lata for
Manas Publications, 4402/5-A,
Ansari Road, (Opp. HDFC Bank),
Darya Ganj, New Delhi-110 002 (INDIA)

Contents

Acknowledgements

The content of Non-formal Education is grounded in the theory and practice of some of the great educational thinkers of our time including Paolo Freire, Howard Gardner, David Kolb, Malcolm Knowles and Bernice McCarthy. This new manual includes information from the previous Peace Corps publications. The Non-formal Education Manual (ICE No. M0042) and The Non-formal Education Training Module (ICE No. T0064) as well as current research from the field of education. In addition to presenting the most current research and thinking in the field of education, the manual also includes field-tested ideas, activities and tips drawn from the experiences of Peace Corps Volunteers and staff around the world.

The Peace Corps recognizes and appreciates the work from the field, contractor, and education specialist and other headquarters staff that made this new publication possible. Gratitude is also expressed to the various writers and publishers who gave permission to reprint and adapt their materials.

INTRODUCTION

Why a Manual on Non-formal Education?

Whether or not you have heard the term non-formal education (NFE) prior to joining Peace Corps, as a Volunteer you will engage in NFE in some way throughout your service. In fact, teachers, extension agents, small business experts, health workers, agricultural specialists—indeed, most people who are involved in "development" in any way—are involved in the sharing of skills and knowledge or changing attitudes, and as such, are engaged in some degree of non-formal education. At the root of NFE is a participatory, grassroots approach to helping people to clarify and address their own needs. In many ways, NFE goes to the heart of what it means to be a Peace Corps Volunteer—a respect for local knowledge, a faith in the wisdom of the people, and a humble awareness of one's own strengths, gifts, and challenges.

This manual is intended to provide both practical skills for engaging in non-formal education and some underlying theory to help you define and develop your own approach to NFE. Based on two previously published Peace Corps resources, Non-formal Education Manual and Non-formal Education Training Module, this resource represents a combination and elaboration of those manuals to bring together the best thinking from the past with the most current approaches in the field of NFE.

Who is this Resource for?

The most obvious audiences for this manual are education Volunteers and those agriculture, business development, environment, health, youth development, and other Volunteers who are called upon to facilitate learning activities in their work, whether for in-school or out-of-school youth, colleagues or other adults. This manual includes ideas for those Volunteers who require theory and practical skills to conduct training workshops and learning activities in their communities and schools. However, NFE is more than an approach to training and session design; and as such, the reach of this manual extends far beyond those leading NFE sessions. NFE provides a powerful philosophy and an effective approach for identifying and creating learning opportunities and facilitating change in a community; therefore, it is an important tool for any Volunteer.

In addition to Volunteers, many other groups will find this manual useful in their work:

- Host country national (HCN) counterparts, including teachers, health workers, agriculture extension agents, business advisors, community leaders, and anyone wishing to work on individual or community development, using respectful, participatory approaches.
- Peace Corps training staff who wish to train Volunteers in non-formal education techniques and approaches, or who want to enhance the NFE aspects of their own facilitation styles.

- Associate Peace Corps Directors (APCDs) who may wish to model NFE approaches for Volunteers and trainees in their projects.

Organization of Each Chapter

Each chapter builds on the theories and activities of the others, so there is some benefit to reading the text from start to finish. But each chapter may also be read as a stand-alone module. Whether you choose to read the book from cover to cover or decide to skim through it for topics that are of particular interest to you, we hope that you will find theories, activities, techniques, suggestions, and lessons learned from other Volunteers, to guide you in developing your own unique approach to NFE.

Pre-reading Strategy

Assess your Knowledge, Skills, and Attitudes

Each chapter begins with a table that outlines the knowledge, skills, and attitudes that you should have to be effective in the capacity described in that chapter. Beneath each KSA, there is a space for you to evaluate your current knowledge, skills, and attitudes, along with an opportunity to create a learning plan to address any gaps in your KSAs.

Reading

This section of each chapter provides important concepts and theories along with vignettes and "lessons learned" about the experiences of Volunteers and HCN counterparts.

Ideas and Applications

Each chapter contains activities to help you practice NFE in training, in your community, or at work. Use the ideas in each of these sections to explore NFE approaches and to develop your own particular style. This section closes with a list of reflective questions to help you process the information.

Key Resources

A number of ICE publications, books, and online resources are listed at the end of each chapter to guide your further study of any of the concepts provided in the text. These resources can help you if you find that you still need to work on any of the KSAs after you have read the chapter.

Chapter – 1

WHAT IS NON-FORMAL EDUCATION?

Pre-reading Strategy

Assess your Knowledge, Skills, and Attitude

The chart below provides you with an overview of the content of this chapter, a chance to reflect on what you already know, and a place to identify those concepts, skills, and attitudes that you want to learn, enhance, or improve.

Before reading the chapter, spend a few minutes with this chart.

1. Review the knowledge, skills, and attitudes listed.
2. Note those you already feel confident about in the row entitled "Your strengths."
3. Note those you wish to study more in the "Your plans to learn more" now. Then use the materials and activities in the chapter to learn in ways that are stimulating and meaningful to you.

	KNOWLEDGE	SKILLS	ATTITUDES
Knowledge, skills, and attitudes useful to NFE	• Definitions of formal, non-formal, and informal education. • Differences between and applications of formal, non-formal and informal education • Distinctions among teacher, trainer, and facilitator • Adult learning theories • Understanding of asset-based and problem-based approaches	• Effective communication • Listening and observation • Identifying cultural factors that impact teaching and learning	• Respect for the knowledge and skills of others • Self-confidence • Patience • Flexibility and adaptability in responding to participants' needs
Your strengths			
Your plans to learn more			

NFE in Action: Peace Corps' Application of Non-formal Education

While the non-formal education approach may seem new to Volunteers who have spent their lives in the formal school system, various manifestations of NFE have been active for centuries in traditional societies. In West African villages and towns as well as in the early United States, young people are apprenticed to local blacksmiths, carpenters, seamstresses, and tailors to learn a trade through firsthand experience or on-the-job training.

In societies as diverse as Nepal, Ghana, and Guatemala, clan and village leaders respected for their age and hereditary status pass on information about agricultural practices; traditional birth attendants educate new mothers in caring for themselves and their babies; and religious leaders impart wisdom through parables, riddles, and the influence of their own personal virtue.

Through dance and song and oral narrative, through puppet theatre and play acting, through one-to-one teaching and group facilitation, people all over the world have used non-formal education methods to pass on traditional knowledge and ensure that each new generation learns the wisdom, harmony, and stability of the old.

The Peace Corps uses non-formal education methods to further its goal of development in people to people terms: helping people develop the capacity to improve their own lives. Although it may seem that development activities center around 'things' such as community gardens, wells, or a school computer lab, the real strength of the project is that the community has learned to identify what they would like to see changed, used their own strengths to do so, and learned new skills to achieve their goals. The flourishing garden is a wonderfully tangible product, but the sustainability of the project lies in the skills and abilities the community has gained through the process. The role of the Volunteer is to work with host country nationals to facilitate the process, and non-formal education methods can be used from the initial assessment stage to the final evaluation and realization of the process and product.

For more information on the role in the Volunteer in development, read the Peace Corps' publication *Roles of the Volunteer in Development: Toolkits for Building Capacity*, Washington, DC: Peace Corps, 2002.

Formal, Non-formal, and Informal Education

Formal Education

For most Volunteers, it is simple enough to relate to the notion of formal education—one gets an image of a classroom and established curricula, teachers, and students with a clearly drawn hierarchy, tests, and milestones. Consider Diane's experience as a new education Volunteer. Although the faces, language, setting, and even her own role may be new to Diane, the situation is comfortingly familiar. After spending at least sixteen years in school systems herself, Diane was quite accustomed to classrooms, tests, and the traditional roles of teachers and students.

DIANE

Diane had never taught school before, but she tried to muster up her courage as she walked through her classroom door that first day on the job at her new post. She tried not to be nervous as she clutched her lesson plan and remembered how well her practice sessions had gone in training. Still, she felt a lot of pressure; after all, how well she taught these students would determine how well they would do on the national exam, and that would determine whether they got into university, and that might make the difference between a life of poverty and a life of hope. So she would have to make sure she covered all of the topics in the curriculum fully so that the students would be able to memorize them all and would do well on the exam. Maybe she would even help them learn some new test taking skills. And hey, she thought, as she locked at the giggling, blushing group of students in front of her, just because we had so much to learn, didn't mean we couldn't have any fun! She swallowed her worries, smiled cheerfully and introduced herself...

At its best, formal education involves a government that recognizes the value of an educated citizenry and supports school systems with curricula designed to meet changing societal needs. Parents and communities are engaged to enhance the impact of motivated and talented teachers who empower enthusiastic youth to acquire the knowledge and skills they need to achieve their goals. When the above elements are not present, the formal education system can seem, at worst, like a warehouse to "store" youth as they grow or the one-way "banking education" Brazilian educator Paulo Freire described. His analogy likened formal education to teachers depositing knowledge into their students' heads, much like depositing money into a bank.

The reality is that most formal education falls somewhere in between Diane's example of a formal education approach and the next discussion of a non-formal education approach. Motivated and talented teachers work in every country, and over the past few decades, ministries of education involved in education reform have supported the evolution and application of more holistic, participatory approaches. Learning objectives, while still designed to meet testing requirements, are also intended to enhance students' capacity for critical thinking, creative problem-solving, and personal growth.

For Peace Corps Volunteers working in the education sector and for other Volunteers conducting health, environment or other lessons in the classroom, this evolution has meant that non-formal education approaches can provide valuable tools in motivating students and designing lesson plans. The goal of Volunteer work in formal education includes addressing curricula requirements using (or training teachers to use) learner-centered, participatory experiences and extra curricular activities that engage students in their own intellectual growth and achievement.

Characteristics of Formal Education

- Usually in a classroom setting, although not just school-based
- Content is usually predetermined by teacher or other person/group in authority (perhaps even the Volunteer)
- Pre-established hierarchy between teacher and student
- Often culminates in a formal test or proof of knowledge

Non-formal Education

While the characteristics of formal education seem self-evident, non-formal education is a bit more difficult to define. In fact, there are many different definitions of NFE, and a number of perspectives about the true meaning of the term.

NFE is defined differently by different practitioners—some say that NFE is any out-of-school learning, others stress that participants need to design their own learning activities, while others say that non-formal teaching methods can be incorporated into all learning. Let's take a look at the work of another Volunteer as we begin to develop our own definition of non-formal education.

As you read about Marisol's experience, reflect on the following:

- Who decided what the women needed to learn?
- Who took responsibility for the learning?
- What resources did each person bring to the experience?
- What kinds of learning activities did the group engage in?
- What was Marisol's role in the small business sessions?

MARISOL

Marisol's assignment was to work with women's groups at village community centers to help them develop small business skills. Since the women rarely had time to come to the community center, Marisol spent a lot of time going from house to house, visiting the women and chatting with them while they did their daily chores.

After four months of listening and observing the women, Marisol felt ready to bring some of them together—the ones who already owned businesses—to help them to upgrade their skills in marketing and management.

The first group consisted of only two women, one who made soap and the other who tie-dyed cloth using indigo that she made from local plants. As the two women became friends, they discovered that both of the small businesses had the same problem: lack of access to a market. However, the soap maker had thought of some clever advertising, and the tie-dyer had a way of reducing her production costs to almost zero. In their conversations they gave each other a few new ideas and came up with a plan to get free transportation to a larger town together on market day.

From this first experience, Marisol discovered that the local women already had most of the expertise they needed between them to improve their sales and management. Slowly, the group grew by word of mouth, and then began to expand to other villages. In group meetings, Marisol stayed in the background, facilitating discussion and sharing among members, arranging for field trips that the women chose themselves and occasionally offering advice on specific business methods.

Think again about the questions posed earlier. Some of the features of non-formal education that you may have identified include:

- **Focuses on the learners' needs:** The women actively identified their own needs and proposed solutions.
- **Uses the learner as a resource:** All of the women, including Marisol, shared knowledge and skills. They were all respected and valued for their contributions.
- **Stresses relevant activities and practical outcomes:** The focus of the learning was the improvement of the women's own lives and that of their families and communities. This was true for Marisol as well, who learned how to make soap and tie-dyed cloth and gained fresh perspective on the lives of the women in her town.

In Marisol's case, the women learned from each other through unstructured discussions. But some non-formal education experiences include more structured activities and training. As you read Tana's Peace Corps' experience below, think about the following:

- How are Marisol's and Tana's experiences similar?
- How are their experiences different?
- What elements of non-formal education are present in Tana's experience?
- What learning activities did Tana use?

TANA

Tana came to a small village in Thailand with seven years of public health experience in the US behind her. As part of her assignment, she was expected to teach prenatal care to the women in the community.

Tana contacted key village leaders and traditional birth attendants, prepared flipcharts and posters with carefully drawn diagrams, and set up meetings to talk about prenatal care to the village women. But to her surprise, only a handful of women turned up at the first meeting. Although she encouraged discussion and asked people for their opinions, nobody spoke up; in fact, most of the women sat with their heads lowered and would not make eye contact with Tana. Tana closed the meeting and went home embarrassed and angry and unsure about her next steps.

Since Tana was not yet fluent enough in the local language to discuss this with anyone in her village, she asked one of her Peace Corps trainers for advice. Endang was sympathetic but pragmatic when he said: "The women you met with weren't protesting learning about prenatal care; they were embarrassed at the way you talked about such a sensitive subject."

Endang reminded Tana of the traditional puppet show she and her training group had attended early in pre-service training. As she talked the problem over with Endang, she learned that puppet shows were the traditional forum for sensitive topics. Puppets could do and say things that flesh and blood people would never discuss openly. Even mixed audiences could discuss the actions of the puppets and learn valuable lessons from them while being entertained.

While Tana knew that to be fully effective she would need to further develop her language skills and gradually become closer friends with the people in the village, she felt that using traditional puppets could get the women talking. Tana returned to her village ready to try this new approach.

Tana's story seems a bit like formal education in some ways. The content has already been determined, and Tana seems to have more of a teacher/trainer role than Marisol. Nevertheless, Tana was engaging in non-formal education.

- How did Tana confront her initial difficulties in reaching the members of her community?
- Think about Tana's discussion with Endang. Why did she seem so open to his feedback and advice? What does this teach us about giving and receiving feedback?
- What do you think will be the overall outcome of the puppet show?

- If Tana does a content appropriate lesson (such as the effects of water pollution) using puppets with students in a high school classroom, would this still be an example of NFE?

As you can see from both of these stories, NFE is an approach to education. It is not absolutely distinct from formal education in its methods; participants exercise varying degrees of control over the process, from designing all of their own learning and using the facilitator as a resource person as in Marisol's story, to attending a learning activity where the content is mostly planned in advance, as in Tana's case. In some ways, we might imagine formal and non-formal education along a continuum—from high to low facilitator control, and from low to high learner participation.

In a nutshell, NFE is an approach to education that can be used with adults, youth, or children, within the classroom or outside of it. An integral part of NFE is that learners participate in the design, development, implementation, and evaluation of their own learning.

Informal Education

If you imagine learning on a continuum, informal education would be at the far end from formal education. We all learn informally every day; it's almost incidental. Learning informally can be as simple as learning a new fact or skill by listening to or observing a friend or colleague, or actively going to the library in search of specific information to suit your needs. Also referred to as "lifelong learning", informal education is usually initiated and the content determined by the individual learner to suit his or her needs as they arise.

Basic Concepts of Adult Learning Theory

The Peace Corps' practice of non-formal education owes much to traditional learning practices, and has been further enhanced through the theory and practice of some of the great educational thinkers of our time. Some of these theorists will be discussed throughout this book, and you might explore others by reading texts suggested in the Key Resources section of each chapter. Some of the most influential thinkers in the field of non-formal education include:

- Paulo Freire

Freire used "problem-posing" methods to raise awareness of social issues and to stimulate action by disadvantaged groups. Using a process of problem analysis, reflection, and action, his approach to education was based on the belief that community members need to be encouraged to think critically about problems in their daily lives in order to make decisions and take action.

- Howard Gardner

Gardner's work on multiple intelligences has had an enormous impact on the field of education. Gardner posits at least seven intelligences (musical, spatial, linguistic, logical/mathematical, bodily/kinesthetic, interpersonal, intrapersonal), and asserts that successful learning experiences should engage as many of these intelligences as possible.

- Malcolm Knowles

Knowles popularized adult learning theory and offered ways to apply it in learning activities. Knowles believed that the needs of adults in education differed a great deal from the needs of children. He popularized the term andragogy, "the art and science of helping adults learn" to draw a sharp distinction between adult learning and pedagogy, the instruction of children. He suggested that because children had yet to assume responsible, independent roles in society, teachers and parents tend to make the decisions about what and how they should learn. But because adults have a wealth of life experience and have already assumed responsible roles, it is important to respect slightly different principles when engaging in adult education. (See Adult Learning Principles inset.)

- David Kolb

Kolb popularized an awareness of learning styles, and created a model that suggests four different categories of learning—concrete experimentation, reflective observation, abstract conceptualization, and active experimentation. Kolb created a methodology for incorporating these four categories into every learning experience—the "experiential learning cycle." His work is described more fully in Chapter 3: Learning Activities: From Assessment to Evaluation.

- Bernice McCarthy

McCarthy expanded on Kolb's work and the research on left and right brain processes to create her 4MAT System. McCarthy suggested four learning types: imaginative learners, analytic learners, common sense learners, and dynamic learners. Her 4MAT System is a thoughtful framework for approaching lesson design, and it is detailed in Chapter 3: Learning Activities: From Assessment to Evaluation.

Adult Learning Principles

Adults:

- Expect to be treated with respect and recognition.
- Want practical solutions to real-life problems.
- Can reflect on and analyze individual experiences.
- Have different learning styles.
- Are motivated by the possibility of fulfilling personal needs and aspirations.
- Are capable of making their own decisions and taking charge of their own learning.

It is probably clear that there are a number of parallels between adult learning theory and our earlier definition of non-formal education. The link between NFE and adult learning theory is so strong, in fact, that many practitioners assert that NFE *is* adult education, and that it cannot be used with children and youth. But consider some of the principles of adult learning listed above. Do you think they also apply to children and youth?

Working with Youth

In many cases, Volunteers will find themselves working on a youth education project within a school or attached to an organization. In these cases, the curriculum is largely predetermined and specific goals must be met by teachers and students. Even though this is a formal education setting, there are many opportunities to use non-formal education methods to assess, inform, and evaluate student progress.

Increasingly, Volunteers may find themselves working with youth who are not attending school. Out-of-school youth differ from in-school youth in several ways. Differences include: more unstructured time, fewer adults providing support and encouragement in a learning environment, more vulnerability to physical and emotional abuse, and more exposure to daily pressures of meeting basic human needs.

Because these youths generally lack the structure other youths have, non-formal education projects can be most beneficial to these often vulnerable populations. Volunteers can act as agents of change by assisting youth to develop critical life skills: identifying their own needs, facilitating information gathering sessions (this could be a more formal lesson given by the Volunteer, a planned group activity or club or a demonstration lesson) and helping them to evaluate their own progress.

For more information on working with youth, refer to the Peace Corps' publication Working with Youth: Approaches for Volunteers, Washington, DC: Peace Corps, 2002.

NFE and CCBI in the Formal Education System

A teacher within the formal education system can easily incorporate non-formal education methods in varying degrees inside the school. Certainly teachers in the formal school system must be responsive to the realities of an established curriculum, protocol, and testing standards, but NFE can be creatively incorporated into any classroom. You can do a quick needs assessment to determine knowledge gaps, or an end of unit evaluation to see if the content was learned and to see if you need to reinforce any information with follow-up lessons. Encourage conversation or energize a sleepy student group with a quick icebreaker activity, or use several different teaching methods to deliver one lesson to reach students with different learning styles. You will learn more about all of these tools in later chapters.

Your familiarity with and ability to employ NFE methods will also help you facilitate Community Content-Based Instruction, or CCBI. CCBI is Peace Corps' adaptation of Content-Based Instruction, which is a way of incorporating culturally appropriate, real-life examples into an existing curriculum so that learning activities are more relevant to students' lives. Using CCBI, you might:

- **Identify the needs of your community with your students:** Perhaps students might conduct a participatory needs assessment and discover that HIV/AIDS is a major issue in the area. (See Chapter 2: Assessing the Situation and Defining your NFE Approach for more information on conducting participatory needs assessments.)

- **Incorporate the topic into syllabus requirements:** For example, students might be required to learn about probability; instead of using a textbook example to work through, their examples and practice might include working through some problems involving HIV infection rates.
- **Plan community action related to the topic:** For example, students might plan an HIV/AIDS awareness campaign, by making posters and hanging them in the community.

NFE methods can help to promote Community Content-Based Instruction within the formal educational system, because it:

- Involves students actively in identifying needs and finding solutions.
- Promotes learning that is practical, flexible, and based on real needs.
- Focuses on improving the life of the individual and/or community.
- Encourages students to assess, practice, and reflect on their learning.

In addition, CCBI remains within the parameters of the formal education system, as the assessment, content of sessions, and application arise out of syllabus requirements. CCBI is a creative and dynamic method for bridging the gap between the school and community needs.

For more information on CCBI, read Community Content-Based Instruction Manual, Washington, DC: Peace Corps, 2004.

Asset-Based and Problem-Posing Approaches

Non-formal education is a rich field, and Volunteers can draw upon a wealth of theories, philosophies and methods in practicing it at their sites—from participatory analysis to project planning and implementation, to evaluation. Two development approaches bear mentioning at the beginning, as you may need to decide early on which philosophy, or what combination of them, you wish to incorporate into your own work with communities. Both philosophies have their place and are most often used in different phases of working with communities.

Asset or Strength-Based Approaches

Asset-based approaches identify and emphasize the *positive* aspects of a community's resources and activities first. Asset-based approaches grew out of the observation that in some settings, problem- and need-focused approaches can overwhelm or depress groups to the point that they become immobilized or fatalistic about the possibility of positive change. Asset-based approaches seek to increase self-efficacy by starting with and building upon what individuals and groups already possess, do, and have accomplished. The emphasis is on identifying and enhancing existing assets, while promoting networking among groups and community members, and de-emphasizing blame for existing problems. As a result, community members feel more hopeful and motivated about their ability to address real needs.

Building Communities from the Inside Out: A Path Toward Finding and Mobilizing a Community's *Assets* has many good activities. See "Key Resources" at the end of this chapter for more information.

A specific type of an asset- or strength-based approach called Appreciative Inquiry, is often used in organizations. Detailed information about Appreciative Inquiry can be found in *The Thin Book of Appreciative Inquiry.* See "Key Resources" at the end of this chapter for more information.

Problem-posing Approaches or Education for Critical Consciousness

Brazilian educator Paulo Freire used "problem-posing" methods to raise awareness of social problems and to stimulate action by marginalized or disadvantaged groups. Through a unique method of asking questions and working in groups, problem-posing education empowers people to take concrete steps toward improving the quality of their lives.

Problem- and asset-based approaches are not mutually exclusive of each other. While conducting an asset-based resource inventory, information regarding "problems" or "deficits" may surface. While conducting a problem analysis, people may focus on "opportunities" or "solutions." All of this information is important to know and use in designing non-formal education activities. In deciding when to use either or both of these approaches, one important consideration is this: how you begin the dialogue influences the energy level and empowerment of the participants. In other words, your first questions are crucial.

For more information, see the Peace Corps' produced publications: *Roles of the Volunteer in Development, Toolkit 1: Volunteer as Learner, and The New Project Design and Management Workshop Training Manual,*

Facilitation Basics

Effectiveness in development work includes being able to communicate with host-country colleagues and community, establishing rapport and trust and listening to what people want and need to do for themselves to positively affect their

well-being. To be able to facilitate discussions among groups of people is a critical skill. Facilitation is a skill that encourages the members of a group to express and discuss their own ideas. A facilitator models good leadership and stewardship but makes sure that the decision-making rights and responsibilities remain with the learners. Facilitators ask questions that elicit ideas, probe, and encourage everyone to participate and express views. They also paraphrase and summarize for clarity and understanding. Good facilitation demands attention to the *process* of the group, including encouraging quiet and reticent people and controlling dominant or disruptive participants.

One important step in fostering effective learning is understanding the subtle similarities and differences in the roles of a teacher, a trainer, and a facilitator. Stop for a minute and reflect on the following words—teach, train, facilitate. What words and images come to mind for each of these?

As a Volunteer you are likely to have opportunities to teach, train, and facilitate learning experiences with your community partners at various times throughout your service. For example, you may find you are called on to teach English lessons, to train community members in assessment techniques, or to facilitate meetings and other community activities. Understanding when and how to serve in these different roles will help you be a more effective Volunteer. In our context of non-formal education, the roles of "facilitator," "trainer" and "teacher" are distinct, although they overlap in several key areas. We distinguish among the three as follows:

- **a teacher** follows set curriculum guidelines (usually dictated at the national level by government agencies) to ensure that all learners assimilate specific subject matter content at an established standard;
- **a trainer** addresses specific requests from individuals or groups for new knowledge and skills relevant to their goals and pursuits; and
- **a facilitator** guides a group through a process of expressing ideas, analyzing issues, making sound decisions, and building relationships.

Clearly, there is a great deal of overlap in these three roles. You may find that, depending on the learning context, the learners, and the learning objectives, you will switch from one role to another during the course of implementing a learning activity. Having a sense of these different roles will help you navigate them more effectively.

Ideas and Applications

Now that you have read about different approaches to education, it may be helpful to apply what you have learned. Feel free to try one, several or all of these activities to practice what you've learned.

What type of Education is it?

Think back on the discussion of the different approaches to education—formal, non-formal, and informal education, and adult learning compared to youth education. Now take a look at the chart below and the accompanying examples. Where would you place each of the examples on the chart? How did you decide where to place the examples? Is each example clearly one approach or another, or does it encompass aspects and characteristics from several of these approaches to education?

Adult		
Youth		
Formal	Non-formal	Informal

A. A student brings a frog into a classroom and the children decide to build a terrarium.

B. A teacher sits with men in the shade and talks about HIV prevention.

C. A Volunteer works with a woman from his or her town to conduct women's literacy classes in the evening.

D. A health worker administers a post-test at the end of a workshop for traditional birth attendants.

E. A Volunteer shows women waiting at a clinic how to make more nutritious porridge.

F. In the classroom, children learn about how waste products can pollute their water. They then take a walk to the nearest well, stream, or other water source to get water samples for testing.

G. Students take an entrance exam for secondary school.

Reflect on Your own Experiences with Non-formal Education

Think back over the many learning experiences throughout your life. List a few examples of non-formal education that you participated in as a *learner*. Identify a particularly memorable experience and analyze it, according to some of these prompts:

I. Where did it take place?

II. Who was involved, as teacher/facilitator/coach?

III. Who were the learners, in addition to you?

IV. How did the learning take place? (demonstration, discovery, practice, etc.)

V. Why was the learning so memorable? (unexpected, something you really needed/wanted to learn, exciting, long-lasting influence, etc?)

Think through this process again, but this time think about an experience where *you* were a facilitator/teacher/coach. What was a particularly exciting or memorable learning experience you helped create for others?

I. Work through questions 1-4 above in relation to that experience.

II. What specific knowledge, skills, and attitudes made you effective?

III. Are you more comfortable in formal or informal teaching situations?

IV. In what ways might you need to adapt your preferred style to meet other opportunities or requirements of your work?

Practice Non-formal Education in Your New Culture

As you begin to develop your own approach to non-formal education, it may be helpful to explore the various approaches to NFE in your new culture. Whether you are still in your training group or already at your new site, consider "shadowing" a health worker, agricultural extensionist, traditional birth attendant, or other community outreach worker for a day or two to observe his or her approach to NFE.

Some questions to explore include:

- What do you notice about the relationship between the educator and the people he or she serves?
- How do they relate to each other?
- What are the approaches to conversation? Is it direct or indirect? Are there differences in communication based on gender, age, status?
- Do men and women participate together or do they tend to move in separate groups?

- Where does the NFE work occur? Does the educator go to people one-on-one in their homes or is there a group-learning opportunity at a community gathering area?
- What specific methods and techniques does the educator use to engage the group?
- What materials are used? Are they available locally? Have they been created by the educator out of local materials? How?
- Picture yourself engaging in the NFE activity. What would you replicate? What would you do differently? Why?
- Does the educator have any recommendations for you as you begin this kind of work? Is there anything to avcid?

Key Resources

References :

Freire, Paulo. *Pedagogy of the Oppressed.* New York: Seabury Press, 1970.

Freire's groundbreaking text suggests powerful possibilities for creating a liberating education. Freire describes the "problem-posing" method to engage participants in a cycle of problem analysis, reflection and action, often through the use of "codes."

Gardner, Howard. *Frames of Mind: The Theory of Multiple Intelligences.* New York: Basic Books, 1993.

Since its original publication in 1983, *Frames of Mind* has served as the seminal text on multiple intelligences. Gardner explores at least seven intelligences—musical, spatial, linguistic, logical/mathematical, bodily/kinesthetic, interpersonal, and intrapersonal—and suggests ideas for creating a "multiple intelligence atmosphere" in a learning environment.

Knowles, Malcolm. *The Adult Learner: A Neglected Species.* Houston, TX: Gulf Publishing Co., 1978.

Published originally in 1973, *The Adult Learner: A Neglected Species* is Knowles' seminal text on the particular needs and learning styles of the adult learner. In it, Knowles popularizes the term "andragogy" and suggests specific approaches for working effectively with adults.

Kolb, David A. *Experiential Learning: Experience as the Source of Learning and Development.* New Jersey: Prentice Hall TPR, 1983.

This text provides the theoretical and practical underpinnings of Kolb's learning styles theory, and introduces the experiential learning cycle. The book also includes Kolb's Learning Styles Inventory (LSI).

McCarthy, Bernice. *The 4MAT System: Teaching to Learning Styles with Right/Left Mode Techniques.* Barrington, IL: EXCEL, Inc., 1987.

McCarthy combines Kolb's theories with research on left and right-mode processing preference to create her 4MAT system. This text provides a concise and clear description to McCarthy's four learning styles and suggests specific approaches for using the 4MAT system to create powerful session plans.

Additional Resources:

Annis Hammond, Sue. *The Thin Book of Appreciative Inquiry.* Plano, TX: Thin Book Publishing Co., 1998.

Gardner, Howard. *Multiple Intelligences: The Theory in Practice.* New York: Basic Books, 1993.

Published ten years after the release of Gardner's theory of multiple intelligences, this text explores the educational applications of MI theory. Using a number of case studies and examples from the field, educators present practical guidance for operationalizing MI theory in various learning situations.

Knowles, Malcolm, et al. *The Adult Learner: The Definitive Classic in Adult Education and Human Resource Development.* Houston, TX: Gulf Professional Publishing, 1998.

This text provides a basic background on Knowles' adult learning theory, along with updated material on the latest advances in the field. The book includes information on learning contracts and a self-diagnostic tool to help assess your own skills as a trainer.

Kretzmann, John P. and John L. McKnight. *Building Communities from the Inside Out A path Toward Finding and Mobilizing a Community's Assets.* Evanston, IL: The Asset-Based Community Development Institute, 1993.

This text offers practical advice, useful tools, and a powerful guide to an asset-based approach to community development. The book suggests ways to map community assets and mobilize these strengths towards building healthier communities.

Recording and Using Indigenous Knowledge: A Manual. New York: The International Institute of Rural Reconstruction, 1996.

This comprehensive guide to working with local communities provides a basic look at assessing, recording, and working with indigenous populations. The text includes case studies, question guides and suggestions for working with groups. It is also available on the web at http://www.panasia.org.sg/iirr/ikmanual/. *Roles of the Volunteer in Development: Toolkits for Building Capacity.* Washington, DC: Peace Corps, 2002.

RVID provides a comprehensive look at the place of the Volunteer in the development process.

Detailing the Volunteer's roles as learner, change agent, co-trainer, co-facilitator, project co-planner, and mentor, RVID provides countless theories, case studies, activities, and approaches to help Volunteers and their communities get the most out of their two years of service.

Vella, Jane. *Learning to Listen, Learning to Teach: The Power of Dialogue in Educating Adults.* San Francisco: Jossey-Bass, 2002.

In this updated edition of her landmark book, Vella revisits her twelve principles of adult education. Using a number of personal examples, Vella describes various approaches to using these principles for respectful teaching of adults all over the world.

Werner, David. *Where There is No Doctor.* Palo Alto, CA: The Hesperian Foundation, 1977. Translated into 80 languages, this text may be the most widely used medical reference in the world. And in addition to its merits as a health resource, Werner's text offers a powerful introduction to adult learning. Werner, David and Bill Bower. *Helping Health Workers Learn: A Book of Methods, Aids, and Ideas for Instructors at the Village Level.* Palo Alto, CA: The Hesperian Foundation, 1982.

Although the title suggests that this book is for health workers at the village level, the messages, methods, teaching techniques, and approaches can be adapted to any learning situation. Werner and Bower effectively describe Freirian participatory approaches to education and provide a wealth of examples and strategies for using these theories in learning situations.

Chapter – 2

ASSESSING THE SITUATION AND DEFINING YOUR NFE APPROACH

Pre-reading Strategy

Assess your Knowledge, Skills, and Attitudes

In any situation where learning activities might be introduced, there are many factors to consider:

- Who has identified the situation to be addressed? The participants? The officials of an organization? Outside experts? You, the Volunteer?
- Is the situation a desired change identified and voiced by the participants (e.g., villagers, health workers, students, farmers, youth group, etc.), a need to be addressed or a problem to be solved?
- Is it something the participants recognize as a need or a problem? Are participants interested in working on it? Do they see it as a priority?
- What has been done about the need or problem in the past – both successfully and unsuccessfully?
- What resources are available?

	KNOWLEDGE	SKILLS	ATTITUDES
Knowledge, skills, and attitudes needed to practice NFE	• Importance of assessment before beginning learning activities or projects • Several tools for assessment	• Community entry skills • Ability to conduct several participatory analysis tools	• Respect for local knowledge, beliefs and priorities • Trust in group process • Patience
Your strengths			
Your plans to learn more			

Exploring what participants want to change or need to change to make their lives better has often been called "conducting a need assessment." However, the concept of "need" must be given perspective. At times, people want things that are not technically needed; there may be some thing, idea, or information they have heard about that they want or desire. In other situations, people may not see as "needs" or "problems" those things that outsiders identify as needs. That is what the community views as a need might not be an issue to an outsider. Likewise, an outsider might identify a "need" but the community may be perfectly content with the status quo. So, as we explore needs and needs assessments, it is important to bear in mind that for learning activities to be effective, the learners must have some motivation to embrace the change. (Recall the principles of adult learning from chapter 1.)

In this chapter we'll explore some different ways of assessing the situations we find, both to educate ourselves and to discover with our learners what they want—and are motivated—to learn.

Reading

NFE in Action: Assessing the Situation

KARLENE AND CHRISTINE

"That does it, we're going home," said Karlene to her husband as she shut the door of their house with as much of a bang as she could. Robert knew she didn't mean it. Both of them had said this off and on to each other over the four months they had been posted to the village.

"What happened today?" asked Robert gently, although he already knew the answer.

"Nothing, that's what happened," said Karlene. "We're getting nowhere."

"Didn't the women's group show up?" asked Robert. "Oh, they were at the community center," said Karlene. "They just didn't want to do anything. I don't know how they want me to help them find ways to earn money, or if they want me to help them at all. Every time I suggest an idea they sort of bat it around for awhile, and then it falls flat."

"So what did you do?" asked Robert.

"We talked. We sat around. We watched people walk by."

"What did you talk about?"

"Oh, marriages, babies. It's incredible how much women's lives here revolve around babies. I don't know where they get the energy. I'm not saying I don't like spending time with the group. You know me, I like babies and marriages. And I know they care about us, too. Remember when they brought us all that food when our garden dried up?"

"I remember," said Robert.

"Nice people," sighed Karlene. "But I wish I knew what I was doing here...I keep wondering if I'm doing something wrong. I mean, look at Christine, she's busy at the clinic. She's already teaching," said Karlene. "She set up a class in the waiting room to explain what foods women ought to be giving their kids. You know, she was telling me the number one problem here is really malnutrition because of the taboos on fish in the coastal villages."

"Does she feel she's making headway?" asked Robert. "Well, it's slow," said Karlene. "She told me she uses the broken record technique. She explains the food pyramid over and over, very slowly, sometimes in story fashion, the way people do here. She's got this great flannel board with cutouts of all the good local foods. At least she'll be busy for her two years here," said Karlene. "What will I have to show for our Peace Corps service?"

There is often a temptation among Volunteers and other development workers to "get to work" right away when coming into a new community or job. It seems easier to figure out what needs to be done and start doing it yourself, rather than spend days, weeks, even months getting to know people, learning about the community and using participatory techniques to discover desires and needs and plan a community-led project. But those projects in which community members have actively identified their own goals and proposed their own solutions are far more likely to lead to sustainable improvements in their lives. This ownership of the project and the process is crucial to the success of any development program, and engaging in participatory analysis is at the crux of what it means to be a practitioner of NFE.

Consider the two quite different experiences of Karlene and Christine:

- Even though Karlene is frustrated, what is she learning about the lives of the women that she is there to help?
- How might Karlene adapt her conversations with the group to help her clarify the possibilities for her work? What else might she do?

- How did Christine determine the content of her training?
- What health concerns do the villagers have?
- How might Christine reconcile her own perceptions with those of the people in her community to create a positive NFE experience?
- Think back to the asset-based and problem-based approaches in Chapter 1:

- How might Karlene have used an asset-based approach in her discussions with the women in her community group to develop a better understanding of their situation?
- How might Christine use the asset-based approach to help women see what resources they have that may lead to healthier children?
- How might Christine have used problem-posing education to help the women in her community see the link between their children's health problems and the taboo on eating fish? How might Karlene have engaged the women at the community center in problem-posing education?

Assess the Situation with your Community Partners

There are a several key moments during your work when a focused assessment is very important:

On your own for community entry: When you first enter a community, using techniques such as participant observation, informal discussions, and interviewing will help you build rapport and gain knowledge that will help you work with your community. This process can take two to six months. Although she didn't recognize it, Karlene was engaging in assessment to some extent, and just needed some guidance for ways to better structure her approach. She also needed to realize that she was not wasting her time; she was building a foundation to prepare herself to meet the needs of her women's group.

(See Peace Corps' publications *Roles of the Volunteer in Development: Toolkits for Building Capacity, "Toolkit 1: Role of the Volunteer as Learner,"* [ICE No. T0005], and Learning Local Environmental Knowledge: A Volunteer's Guide to Community Entry, [ICE No. T0126] for more information and approaches to community entry.)

- **With a community group to raise awareness:** Some participatory tools such as daily activity schedules and seasonal calendars are particularly effective in raising awareness about the inter-relatedness of social, health, labor,

economic, and environmental aspects of life. These types of activities not only provide important information but also may offer new perspectives on daily life and often inspire action. For example, Christine might use a seasonal calendar activity to raise the women's awareness of the relationship among illness, nutrition, climate, and other factors.

- **With a community group for project planning:** Careful initial assessment of the situation is crucial when working with a community group to decide what issues will be addressed by a new project. Each member of the group should feel like a stakeholder, with the Volunteer acting as facilitator to be sure that all voices can be heard. A daily activity schedule might be helpful to determine the most convenient time for a representative group of people to meet.

- **Before a planned learning activity or training workshop:** It is important to assess the current knowledge, skills, and attitudes of participants before planning and conducting a learning activity or training workshop. Possible techniques include interviewing, group discussion, and even pre-testing. The data gathered are analyzed to inform the design of the educational event.

A NOTE ON "COMMUNITY"

"Community" in this manual refers to more than those people living in a geographic location. It can refer to any group of people gathered together, whether in schools, institutions, neighborhood groups or affinity groups. "Community" might refer to heterogeneous groups (women from all classes) as well as homogeneous groups (all teen mothers).

Tools for Facilitating Needs Assessments

There is a rich body of experience in conducting participatory needs assessments upon which Volunteers may draw in beginning their work. Some effective approaches to assessment can be found in the Key Resources section at the end of this chapter.

Peace Corps has brought together a number of tools in the development of participatory analysis for community action (PACA). PACA is a methodology designed to communicate information, identify needs, and lay the groundwork for community action to solve problems. The PACA Idea Book [ICE No. M0086] is a valuable resource for conducting needs assessments, as it describes a number of tools and provides advice regarding their use. These tools can be useful and applicable to non-formal education activities as well, and they are summarized for your use.

Observation

Observation is perhaps the one assessment tool that everyone uses. It is only natural when you come into a new situation to begin observing, comparing, analyzing, and trying to make sense of what you see. Observation is an important part of your entry into the community, and as Volunteers you will usually be engaging in participant observation, or sharing in the lives and activities of the community, so that you can learn from experience and observation.

> ***"When you come into a village, your eyes and ears should be open, and your mouth should be closed."***
>
> ***–West African proverb***

Because it is so important to understand the complexities of your new situation before helping people to take any kind of action, it is a good idea to begin to train yourself to observe and reflect with more precision. Here are some suggestions for getting the most out of your observations:

- **Keep a journal:** Write down your observations and impressions to capture, analyze, and compare them over time.
- **Sequential reporting:** Write down exactly what happens as it is happening. Try to be as objective as possible. Avoid interpreting events or making judgments. By forcing yourself to focus on details that you would normally ignore, questions might emerge that you can later follow up on through interviews and other types of observations.
- **Reporting of selective themes:** After doing a number of detailed sequential observations, try following a theme that interests you. Choose a theme or question and write

short notes about it whenever you learn something about it. If you are looking at how much agricultural work women do, you might list every farm activity you see them engaged in and describe those activities. Try to be objective and describe what you see, rather than just capturing your impressions of what you see.

- **Detailed description of an event:** You may witness an interesting incident when it would be insensitive to pull out a pencil and paper. Train yourself to remember as many details as possible to write down later. For example, if you see a woman harnessing cattle in a culture where women do not ordinarily handle animals, mentally note everything about the scene: the time of day, the clothes she was wearing, her ease or discomfort working with the animals and so on. These details will help you question your counterpart more intelligently later about how to interpret what you saw.
- **Subjective observation:** Here you can dispense with the timing, counting, and recording of details and try to capture feelings, relationships, beauty, sadness, the setting, and atmosphere. The color of new rice seedlings at sunrise, the grief of a buffalo driver when his animal collapses and dies on the roadside—these moments cannot be broken down into details and statistics. Use care in your interpretations,

It is important to remember that our perceptions of any event, situation, or person are conditioned by a number of filters. Our own gender, age, personal background, cultural origin, class background, prejudices, beliefs, etc., will affect what we pay attention to, how we perceive what we have seen, and the decision we make about the situation. For example, because she was so determined to focus on nutrition, Christine did not see other community needs, interests, or assets. Karlene's desire to *do* something made it difficult for her to accept "watching and waiting" as valuable approaches.

Your time with Peace Corps has probably helped you to become more aware of the lenses through which we tend to view things, and it is especially important to revisit these issues when conducting observations. See *Culture Matters: The Peace Corps Cross-Cultural Workbook* [ICE No. T0087] for more insight about these "filters."

though, and draw on the knowledge and skills you have gained in doing the previous observations so as not to jump to conclusions.

Shadow Days

One of the most powerful ways to engage in participant observation is to "shadow" a host country national colleague or friend. "Shadowing" involves following the person around throughout the day and engaging (to the extent possible) in the same activities that he or she does. This is a particularly effective technique when attempting to get "on-the-job" training for your technical area. For example, you can learn a great deal about local agricultural techniques by shadowing a local farmer, and you can gain a wealth of information about women's health by shadowing a maternal and child health coordinator at a hospital. By using a combination of observation and shadowing, Christine might be able to assist women in determining their health needs in a non-threatening way, while also integrating into the community.

Informal Discussion

Talking with a great variety of people and asking friendly, culturally appropriate questions can yield useful information. Below are some things to consider when devising and asking questions:

- **Factual Questions:** People may feel intimidated or embarrassed by questions that require specific answers, especially if they do not know the answers. Examples include: "What is the population of this area?" or "How many children are malnourished in this community?" It may be best to leave such questions for interviews with officials in a position to know that information.

- **General Questions:** Try to keep your questions relevant to people's own experience. Instead of asking questions like: "What foods are usually given to children?" try asking: "What do you feed your child every day?"
- **Opinion Questions:** Some questions calling for an opinion may be politically sensitive. For example: "What do you think of the government's new plan for free primary school education?" Save these questions until you feel you know your audience well, and do not press people for answers if you find them being politely evasive. This may be their way of telling you that your questions are inappropriate.
- **Personal Questions:** Even if your work is in sexually transmitted infection (STI) prevention, be careful when asking personal questions. It is crucial to understand the appropriate time, context, and approach to asking personal questions, and it is probably best to rely on your counterpart for guidance in this area.

Key Informants

Finding key informants who will give you specific information may be important both to show respect to local authorities and to get a more complete view of the situation. For example, local health officials may have access to useful documentation that might take you months to collect on your own. Even children may be useful key informants about school-related matters, or as candid translators for their parents who may speak a local language you have not yet mastered.

Your experience may be more effective and enjoyable if you focus on making friends within the community, rather than merely approaching people for "informal discussion" as a needs assessment technique. By engaging in participant observation at football matches, churches and mosques, at community centers, by the water, and so on, you will make friends in the community and will be able to casually learn the answers to your questions from them. Sometimes the best "key informants" are close host country national friends who agree to share knowledge with you that is usually not provided to "outsiders."

Remember, though, that each person's view is likely to be very different from that of the next. When discussing the problem of children's malnutrition, for example, one Volunteer found that while everyone she talked to agreed it was a problem, there was much disagreement about its cause.

- A doctor claimed it was caused by the ignorance of the people due to cultural biases against modern medicine.
- The traditional healer said it was the invasion of foreign culture that damaged children's health.
- Teachers felt that the high illiteracy rate prevented parents from reading about nutrition, gardening, and better health practices.
- The agricultural extension agent said it was the lack of inexpensive appropriate technology that could help people produce food year-round instead of just in the rainy season.
- An official from a local aid agency insisted that the children's malnutrition was caused by endemic intestinal parasites because there was no clean water supply in the village.
- Although each of the people the Volunteer talked to understood that many factors contributed to the problem, each person's perspective was different depending on their professional interest and personal bias.

Interviews

Sometimes a formal interview is more appropriate than a casual discussion. The village chief, the leaders of women's groups, the local ministry officials and other professionals may be more amenable to an interview than to informal questioning. Interviews are sometimes useful with community members as well because they are more structured than ordinary conversation and therefore yield more comparable data. Be sure to ask permission of informants to quote them and inform them clearly of your purpose in interviewing them.

Before you conduct an interview, try to find out the culturally sensitive way to go about it. For example, in the culture in which you work:

- Should you avoid eye contact, or is it more polite to look directly at a person?
- How formally or informally should you dress when doing an interview?
- How much time should you spend on greetings and initial chit-chat before beginning the interview?
- Is it appropriate to approach an elder or chief directly, or should you go through intermediaries?
- What subjects or ways of asking questions are considered inappropriate?

What type of interview is best?

This depends both on the situation and on you. Below are some issues to consider when deciding which interview type is best:

- **Language ability:** If you are interviewing in a language you feel unsure of, you might want to use a closed quantitative interview, so that you may write down your questions in advance, check your grammar with an informant and gather information from a pre-written list. Alternatively, you may wish to work with an HCN counterpart in conducting all of the interviews, in which case you might be able to use a standard openended interview or appreciative interview. If your language ability is good, you might want to engage in an informal interview or interview guide approach.
- **Importance of compiling information for analysis:** You might want to use a more structured approach in order to compile your information more efficiently. For example, if

you need to find out what fifty families eat in the rainy season, it would be relatively easy to look at, say, the answers to question six of your interview form and tabulate the results.

- **Desire for holistic picture:** If you want to find out what people feel about a situation, it may be more appropriate to let the interview questions arise naturally in the course of the conversation. Afterwards, when compiling the information, you will need to read the whole batch of interviews over and over again to let a global picture emerge. This can be time-consuming of course, but it will yield a rich, full picture of the range of opinions, perceptions, and styles of expression of your informants. When sharing this kind of information with others it is wise to explain that your own analysis of it will naturally be somewhat colored by your own perceptions and point of view. Or better yet, be sure to read, compile, and analyze the data with HCN counterparts or members of the community.

Now that you have the information, what do you do with it?

Use it for your own education: Interview information, like detailed observations, can help you understand your host country more fully. If you have used informal interviews or an interview guide approach, typing them up or recording the most interesting bits in a journal will help you focus on what people were trying to communicate to you. You can tabulate and record information from more structured types of interviews in the form of charts or graphs, or just as trends to remember for future conversations. For example: "I find it interesting that according to teachers in this town, the main health problem of their students is respiratory infection."

Share it with your co-workers: Ideally, you and your counterparts will gather information together, but if you conduct interviews on your own, you may find it useful to share this new information with others—that is, if it is new to everyone, rather than just to you. Try not to annoy HCNs by acting as an expert on their own society—even if you have found out information that is not common knowledge. People may be put off if you take on the role of expert without being asked.

However, if you are asked to give a presentation, or if you are questioned at a meeting about the information you have been gathering, present it as concisely and accurately as possible, using notes you have taken about the data you have compiled as well as graphs or charts when they seem appropriate.

Share it with the people you have interviewed: The relatively new field of participatory research stresses dialogue, empathetic sharing of experience, and involvement of the people in all phases of information gathering and utilization. Such an approach is consistent with NFE values, for it involves working with people rather than treating them as research "subjects." Try to share the results of your interviews with people at community meetings or other local forums in the oral style that the local people use themselves. You will need to observe awhile to understand the complexities of this style according to the custom in your area. Some cultures are much more indirect about making a point than Americans are, so try to avoid giving "the facts and nothing but the facts" as you may have been trained to do by your own society. It may be that your host country co-workers will be more effective than you in this role and should present the results of your information-gathering to the community.

Community Mapping

The community mapping technique is a highly participatory needs assessment tool in which participants draw or construct maps of their community on paper or on the ground. Subgroups are usually asked to draw separate community maps. For example, the men in the group may work on one map, the women another, the girls another, the boys another. Or adults might work on one map, and youth on another. This tool can visually show significant differences in how these subgroups view their community, how they locate different activities spatially, and how they attribute importance to different activity centers such as schools, markets, clinics and so forth. It can also identify how frequently people are at various locations, places they like and dislike and what they feel is needed or missing in the community. Once this activity is finished, it is often difficult to overlook the differences among the perceptions of men, women, girls, and boys in a community. Now, think back to Tana's experience teaching prenatal care in Thailand from the first chapter.

- How might she have used community mapping to discover the perspectives of women and men around the topic of prenatal care?
- How might she have used this technique to raise awareness about prenatal care services available?

Daily Activity Schedules

In this activity, participants (usually men, women, girls, and boys) create a timeline of their daily activities. This information provides valuable insights into both the labor constraints of each group as well as the areas where labor-saving might occur. At another level, this technique demonstrates the gender-based perceptions of the work load of each group. In this sense, this technique helps to raise awareness with regard to the contribution that different groups make to overall household welfare. Finally, the information developed can serve as baseline data to return to as a way to monitor the impact of project activities on people's time allocations.

- How might Karlene have used daily activity schedules with the women at the community center? What information might she and the women have discovered together during this process?
- How might you incorporate daily activity schedules in your own work?

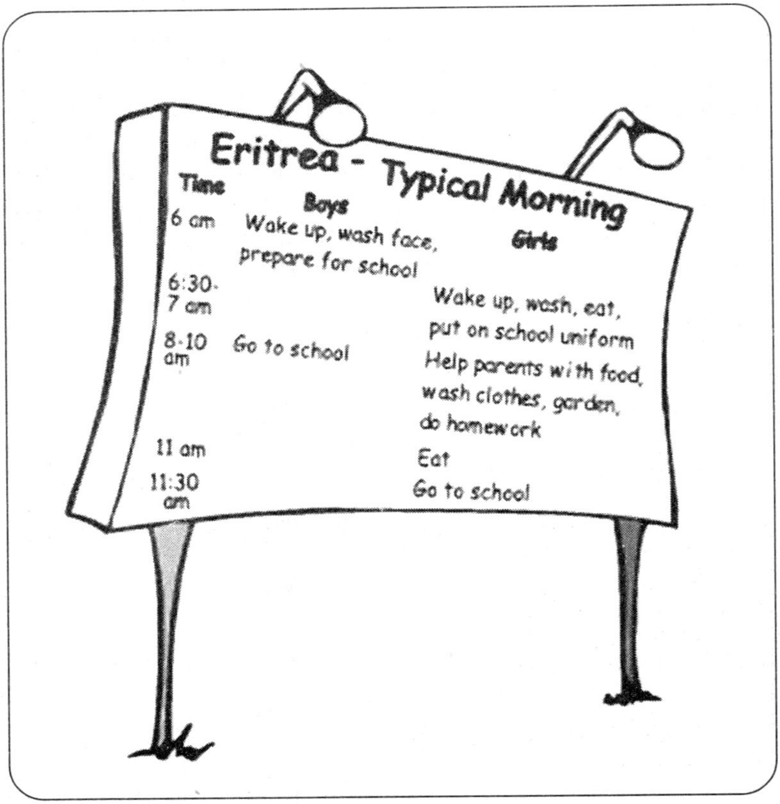

Seasonal Calendars

This technique traces seasonal variations in household labor supply and demand, income flow and expenditure patterns. Many households experience a "hungry season" or periods of economic stress, and these variations may have differential impacts on different gender groups. Some times of the year are busier for one group or the other. This technique is designed to identify these seasonal variations in household well-being from the perspective of both men and women. An understanding of these seasonal variations is important to the development and implementation of a community action plan.

Might seasonal calendars have been helpful to Christine in raising awareness about protein deficiency?

On-the-spot Assessments in Training Situations

You may find that you do not always have the luxury of conducting a thorough needs assessment. You may be asked to conduct a training or class on short notice, or you may find that the participants who get involved in a project or training are different from the people you originally interviewed. Whatever the reason, it is always wise to conduct an on-the-spot assessment. Such an assessment can help you to:

- Engage the participants in the task at hand.
- Clarify expectations and objectives of the project or training.
- Check that your assumptions and conclusions about local needs are still accurate.
- Adjust the agenda or objectives as needed.

For complete instructions on how to use all of the techniques mentioned above, refer to the *PACA Idea Book*, Washington, DC: Peace Corps, 1996.

Ideas and Applications

Now that you have read about assessing learners' needs, it may be helpful for you to apply what you have learned. In this section, you will find several ideas and activities to assist you in practicing what you have learned. Feel free to try one, several or all of these activities. You could also create your own!

Visit a Local Development Organization or Community Group

With so many needs assessment approaches and techniques to choose from, it can be difficult to decide which one might be the most effective or the most culturally appropriate for your own situation. A visit to a local development organization or community group may provide some answers and ideas. Find a local group that uses a participatory approach, and ask what techniques they use in their own assessments. Such groups can often provide guidance when designing your own approach, and may even provide you with some material for use in your work.

Some questions you might ask while on your visit include:

- What cultural norms and taboos should I be aware of when conducting needs assessments?
- What is the protocol for interviewing local leaders? Government representatives? Women? Youth?
- What approaches to conducting needs assessments have you found most useful?
- What methods are used for people with limited literacy?
- Have you recently conducted a needs assessment in this community? Is it possible for me to read some of the results?

Conduct a Participatory Needs Assessment

Whether you are at your pre-service training or already at your site, consider conducting a participatory needs assessment, such as community mapping, daily activity schedules or seasonal calendars. Gather a group of language trainers and guide them through a needs assessment to determine what skills they have and what skills they would like to develop. Or, if you work with a youth group, facilitate a participatory needs assessment to determine what skills they would like to learn.

Case Study: Who Determines Needs in Development?

As you read this case study, consider the following questions:

- What needs assessment approaches were used?
- Do you think the results and conclusions are valid? Why? Why not?
- Would you consider either of these approaches to needs assessment effective? Why or why not?

Food for Thought

A university professor in Washington, D.C. broke her small class of students into two small teams of four for a teambuilding activity. She gave each team 30 minutes to prepare a mock grant proposal to present to a major grant-making foundation to secure funding to realize that group's vision to provide support to AIDS orphans. After a few minutes of scratching heads at the huge task ahead and the small amount of time, the groups got to work.

Proposal One:

Group One's spokesperson outlined a very specific proposal in which the group would form a nonprofit organization based in Washington, D.C. The organization would establish a skeleton staff in Washington, D.C., consisting of an executive director, a program manager, a proposal writer, and a communications manager. This group would manage and oversee the construction of a home for youth in the target country of South Africa. The home would serve youth who had lost both parents due to HIV/AIDS and had no extended family to care for them. The home's capacity would be 50 youth. The proposal described a vibrant, safe community for youth where they would receive the counseling and attention necessary to enable them to enter the workforce as healthy and adjusted members of the community. Therefore, the services the home would provide would include:

- education (academic instruction, vocational services and leadership development);
- health (preventative health, medical and mental health services); and
- room and board.

This group also proposed that the home establish a scholarship fund, so that youth who "graduate" from the home could pursue a university degree. The residents of the home would be involved in every aspect of the fundraising and management of the scholarship fund to impart important leadership skills and to help the youth form links within the community.

Proposal Two:

The spokesperson from the second group requested a different type of funding. The group proposed that before they requested a grant for a specific project, they would request a research grant so that they could go into the specified community and assess the needs within the community. Once in the community, a small research team would assess and interview various community members to gather information. Some preliminary questions they proposed asking:

- What organizations (e.g., non-governmental organizations, faith-based groups, etc.) are currently providing services to AIDS orphans? What kinds of services are they providing? If they could provide other services, what would they be?
- Are there any schools, clinics, or hospitals that currently provide services for this target group?
- What does the AIDS orphan population "look" like? How many are there? Who are they? What is the age range of the children? Where do they currently live? Are they in school or out of school?
- What are the most pressing needs that the orphans have that an outside group should consider funding or providing through services?
- What are the attitudes of various members of the community toward the orphans?
- What knowledge, skill, and belief systems currently exist about HIV/AIDS?

The group also suggested interviewing people who are currently serving as caretakers/guardians for orphans (grandparents, aunts, uncles, etc.). Once some baseline qualitative and quantitative information was captured, the group felt that they would be better positioned to create goals and objectives for a proposal, and to support their request for funds with realistic numbers. Additionally, the group explained that it could use the initial baseline information to more accurately measure progress.

Questions:

Which of these proposals do you think would be most likely to get funded, and why?

If you were going to provide feedback to each of the groups about their approach to needs analysis, what would you say? What are the positive points of each proposal?

Reflect

- Why is it important to conduct needs assessments before planning an educational activity?
- How might you incorporate needs assessment tools into your work?
- Some communities have been assessed and analyzed by development organizations for years. There is already a great deal of data about these communities, and community members have often participated in a number of the tools and techniques mentioned in this chapter. Do you think it is still important to conduct a needs assessment in such a community? How would you go about it?
- Think back on the discussion of asset-based and problem-based approaches. What are the implications of designing and conducting needs assessments?

Key Resources

References :

Culture Matters: The Peace Corps Cross-Cultural Workbook. Washington, DC: Peace Corps, 1997.

A powerful introduction to cross-cultural understanding, Culture Matters explores communication, locus of control, personal versus societal obligations, the concept of time, work culture, and many other issues to consider when living and working in a new cultural environment. A number of activities are provided to help the Volunteer to adjust to the new culture and workplace.

Learning Local Environmental Knowledge: A Volunteer's Guide to Community Entry. Washington, DC: Peace Corps, 2002.

Learning Local Environmental Knowledge is a guide to the first few months of service for Volunteers in all sectors. The text suggests strategies and opportunities for integrating into the community, focusing on the biophysical, economic, and social environments of the area. Combining assessment strategies with personal reflection, this useful guide is a must-read for the new Volunteer.

PACA: Participatory Analysis for Community Action. Washington, DC: Peace Corps, 1996.

Peace Corps' seminal text in assessment, the PACA Idea Book details a number of participatory approaches to assessment, including examples, diagrams, and suggestions for implementation.

Roles of the Volunteer in Development: Toolkits for Building Capacity. Washington, DC: Peace Corps, 2002.

This text provides a comprehensive look at the place of the Volunteer in the development process. Detailing the Volunteer's roles as learner, change agent, co-trainer, co-facilitator, project co-planner, and mentor, RVID provides countless theories, case studies, activities, and approaches to help Volunteers and their communities get the most of out their two years of service. The text includes a number of ideas for conducting assessments.

Additional Print Resources:

Archer, David, and Sara Cottingham. *REFLECT Mother Manual: Regenerated Freirean Literacy through Empowering Community Techniques.* Somerset, United Kingdom: ACTIONAID, 1996.

Grounded in the approaches of Paulo Freire and merged with participatory rural appraisal, this manual details culturally appropriate participatory approaches to assessment. The text also contains a number of activities to help explore power relations with groups.

Chambers, Robert. *Rural Development: Putting the First Last.* University of Sussex, Brighton, United Kingdom: Institute of Development Studies, 1997.

Chambers provides an analysis of biases in development practices, including assessments such as surveys and questionnaires. The text suggests a new framework for working with communities, based on an understanding of rural people's knowledge and reversals in ways of learning, managing, and working with local populations.

De Negri, Berengere, et al. *Empowering Communities: Participatory Techniques for Community- Based Programme Development. Volume 1(2): Trainer's Manual* (Participant's Handbook). Washington, DC: Centre for African Family Studies/USAID, 1998.

This two-volume set details an 18-session training design for teaching PLA (the participatory learning and action approach), facilitation skills, and assessment. Various assessment strategies are detailed, including transect walks, mapping, time lines, card sorting, ranking and diagramming.

Community Content-Based Instruction Manual. Washington, DC: Peace Corps, 2002.

In addition to detailing an approach for working with students in the formal education system, the CCBI Manual suggests a number of participatory assessment techniques to use with student groups.

Idea Book Series: *HIV/AIDS: Integrating Prevention and Care into your Sector*. Washington, DC: Peace Corps, 2002.

This Idea Book offers some practical strategies for assessing and responding to the effects of HIV/ AIDS on each of Peace Corps' project areas. The text offers specific questions to consider when assessing the impact of HIV/ AIDS on each sector.

Kretzmann, John P. and John L. McKnight. *Building Communities from the Inside Out: A path Toward Finding and Mobilizing a Community's Assets*. Evanston, IL: The Asset-Based Community Development Institute, 1993.

This text offers practical advice, useful tools, and a powerful guide to an asset-based approach to community development. The book suggests ways to map community assets and mobilize these strengths towards building healthier communities.

Srinivasan, Lyra. *Tools for Community Participation: A Manual for Training Trainers in Participatory Techniques*. Washington, DC: PROWWESS/UNDP, 1990.

In this classic text, Srinivasan describes her SARAR approach to practicing NFE: using the characteristics of self-esteem, associative strengths, resourcefulness, action planning, and responsibility. Srinivasan advocates a learner-centered approach and specific techniques that she used effectively in working with women around water and environmental sanitation.

Working with Youth: Approaches for Volunteers. Washington, DC: Peace Corps, 2002.

This informative guide to working with youth includes a comprehensive section on participatory assessment. Techniques include Venn diagrams, informal interviews, group interviews, community mapping and tips for compiling information. The text also includes a session on participatory planning.

Chapter – 3

LEARNING ACTIVITIES: FROM ASSESSMENT TO EVALUATION

Pre-reading Strategy

Assess your Knowledge, Skills, and Attitudes

There will come a time when your assessment will indicate the need to engage in some type of teaching—whether it is a one-hour discussion or a weeklong training. Or, perhaps you are a teacher who holds classes every day or a health worker who is called upon to facilitate a few activities a week. In these situations, non-formal education provides a valuable approach to learning by offering models, philosophies, and techniques that:

- involve participants actively in identifying needs and finding solutions;
- promote learning that is practical, flexible, and based on real needs;
- focus on improving the life of the individual and/or community;
- and encourage participants to assess, practice, and reflect on their learning.

	KNOWLEDGE	SKILLS	ATTITUDES
Knowledge, skills, and attitudes needed to practice NFE	• Understanding of learning styles • Knowledge of learning theories • Understanding of group dynamics • Knowledge of principles of and options for learning activity, design and evaluation • Basic knowledge of learning topic	• Ability to assess participant learning styles • Ability to select, develop and implement an appropriate evaluation (when and how) • Ability to design learning activities to address different learning styles • Ability to write behavioural objectives	• Trust in people and their capacities to learn from experience • Self-awareness of your own learning preference • Respect for other learning preferences • Flexibility • Belief that facilitators are also learners • Belief in the importance and value of planning • Willingness to learn from mistakes
Your strengths			
Your plans to learn more			

Fundamental to the NFE approach is the facilitator's belief that he or she is also a learner in the process, and that the participants or students have as much to offer as they have to gain. Keeping this belief central in the creation of a learning activity can result in truly transformational learning experiences—participatory exercises, engaging approaches, and empowering interpersonal interactions. It is also helpful to have an understanding of learning styles, some knowledge about lesson design, and a "toolbox" of warm-ups, exercises, and methods to keep learning activities interactive and engaging. This chapter offers an introduction to all of these topics and suggests further reading in Key Resources at the end of the chapter.

Reading NFE in Action: Recognizing Individual Learning Styles

TRACY

Tracy had always liked fiddling with mechanical things, so when the new refrigeration unit in the health clinic broke down, she volunteered to take it apart and see what was wrong. If the men working around the clinic in her village in Micronesia were amused, they kept it to themselves. They didn't know how to fix the unit, but they knew that the perishable medicines that were flown in so infrequently would spoil if it wasn't fixed somehow. The men glanced at Tracy and shook their heads as she slowly made sense of all the small, greasy refrigerator pieces by studying the diagrams in the refrigerator repair manual.

When the unit was working again, Tracy had its inner mechanisms completely figured out in her head. She could see each piece in relation to the others, like a three-dimensional jigsaw puzzle. It was beautiful, she thought, the way it all went together.

Tracy's supervisor was pleased. In fact, he said Tracy's skills could undoubtedly be put to use on some of the other islands where technical know-how was lacking. He arranged to send Tracy on a trip to teach refrigeration repair to clinic workers in every village where the new units had been installed. At her first stop, Tracy asked the clinic administrator if she could borrow the refrigerator. If Paul, the maintenance person, could take the unit apart, she reasoned, he would understand how it all went together as clearly as she had. Permission was granted, and Tracy sat down on the floor with Paul. She suggested that he take the unit apart, and put it back together again. Paul followed her instructions without saying much, but finally he said: "I'm never going to figure this out. Can you just show me what you did?" For a moment, Tracy was confused. She thought she understood adult learning. Her plan seemed to be such an easy, hands-on way to solve a practical problem. Adults were interested in hands-on experience to solve practical problems, right?

Learning Styles

Tracy's approach to teaching is quite common—it is not unusual to assume that everyone learns the same way that you do. But in reality, there are a number of different ways of learning, and different people learn in different ways. In the 1970s, educator David Kolb popularized this fact and created a model that suggests four different categories of learners. See if you can recognize your own style of learning in the following descriptions.

Kolb's Learning Styles

People who learn best by concrete experience, according to Kolb, make judgments based on feelings or intuition, rather than on theory, which they often dismiss as being "unrelated to real life" or "too abstract." They are people-oriented and often relate more easily to peers than to authority figures. They benefit most from feedback and discussion with other participants who prefer this same mode of learning.

- How might Tracy have adapted her teaching style to meet the needs of people who learn best by concrete experience?

Learners who are most comfortable with reflective observation are more tentative and prefer to listen, think, and stand back before making judgments or consolidating their learning. According to Kolb, they seem introverted in learning situations compared to their more active peers because they enjoy listening to lectures or to others' opinions while they take on the role of impartial, objective observers.

- How might Tracy have met the needs of a reflective observer? What specific learning activities might she have used?

Those who are comfortable with abstract conceptualization tend to be thought of as "logical" and "objective" by their friends and may seem dispassionate or withdrawn in a learning situation. Kolb suggests that they tend to be oriented more towards things and symbols and less toward their peers. They learn best from authority figures in an impersonal environment.

- What specific learning activities might appeal to those who learn through abstract conceptualization? How might the refrigeration repair lesson be adapted for these learners?

Active experimenters learn best when they tackle a project with their hands, often working in groups. Like those who learn best from concrete experience, they are extroverts, but instead of approaching each problem as a special case, they formulate hypotheses and actively test them out. Kolb suggests that they dislike lectures and other passive learning situations.

- What learning style do you think Tracy preferred? Paul?
- Can you identify your own learning style from Kolb's categories?

Kolb points out that individual learners are unlikely to find themselves accurately characterized by just one of these four learning modes. This is because everyone learns by a combination of methods, drawing from all four of these categories. However, people can be characterized as dominantly one type of learner or another. Therefore, in any group, there are likely to be people who are comfortable with quite diverse methods of learning.

Although Tracy's dominant mode of learning may be active experimentation, she may not fit easily into any single category described by Kolb. Other theorists have grouped learners differently: right-brained (artistic) and left-brained (analytic), for example, or auditory or visual. You may remember from Chapter 1 that Howard Gardner's multiple intelligence theory postulates seven different learning styles: linguistic, musical, logical-mathematical, spatial, bodily-kinesthetic, intrapersonal and interpersonal. It is clear from the work of Kolb and Gardner that the most effective learning experience incorporates activities that engage several learning styles.

How might Tracy have designed the refrigerator repair training to accommodate more learning styles? One way would be to incorporate several teaching techniques into a single activity. Tracy might have:

- prepared a demonstration lesson
- presented a mini-lecture
- created a step-by-step hand-out or trouble-shooting guide

Based on your understanding of Kolb's learning styles, which of the above techniques would be best for which types of learners?

Another way Tracy could structure her teaching would be to explore learning styles in the Micronesian culture. Think about the learning styles you have observed at your site so far. Can you draw any conclusions about learning styles in this culture? Ask yourself these questions as you continue to observe learning styles in your community:

- How do children learn their daily chores?
- Do people traditionally observe and imitate when learning new skills?
- How do farmers exchange information?
- Do people take apprenticeships?
- How is local history shared?

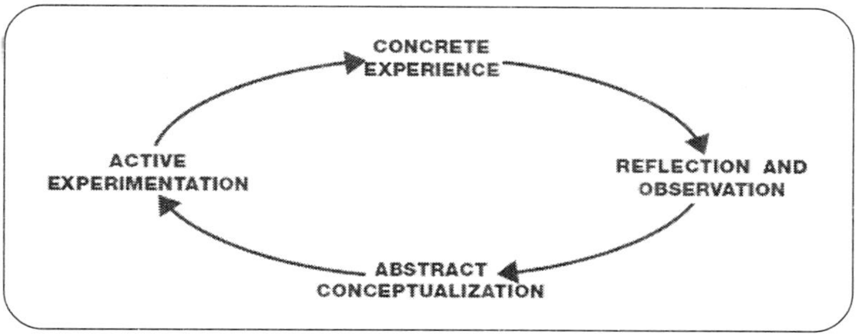

Experiential Learning Cycle

Kolb created a methodology for incorporating all four categories of learning styles into every learning experience. His "experiential learning cycle" models a technique for helping learners to analyze each experience in order to understand it and apply it in their own lives.

Whether we are aware of it or not, each of us moves through these steps in our own daily learning.

- First, you have an experience. For example, in pre-service training you might observe your host family serving considerably more food to the father of the family than to the mother and children.
- Next, you reflect upon the experience. You may ask yourself why the father in the family gets more food than the mother or the children.
- Then, you begin to analyze what is happening. You may attempt to generalize from what you have seen by asking yourself: "Why is this happening?" In the case of your host family, you may decide that fathers are given more food for cultural reasons, or because it is believed that a healthy father leads to more work in the fields which leads to healthier crops which leads to more food for the whole family.
- Lastly, you may begin to apply what you have learned to new experiences. Perhaps you may begin to offer more food to the father of the family yourself, or perhaps you may use this experience to develop programs on nutrition for women and children.

In keeping with his learning styles theory, Kolb believed that people are more adept at learning from some stages of the cycle than they are from others. Some of us have experience after experience and hardly reflect on them at all. Some of us reflect a great deal, but shy away from experiencing anything too unusual. Others reflect and generalize, but stop there, without applying the learning to new situations. Kolb suggests that educators can facilitate learning by consciously taking participants through the entire cycle of experience, reflection, generalization, and application.

You can remember the experiential learning cycle easily if you think of it this way:

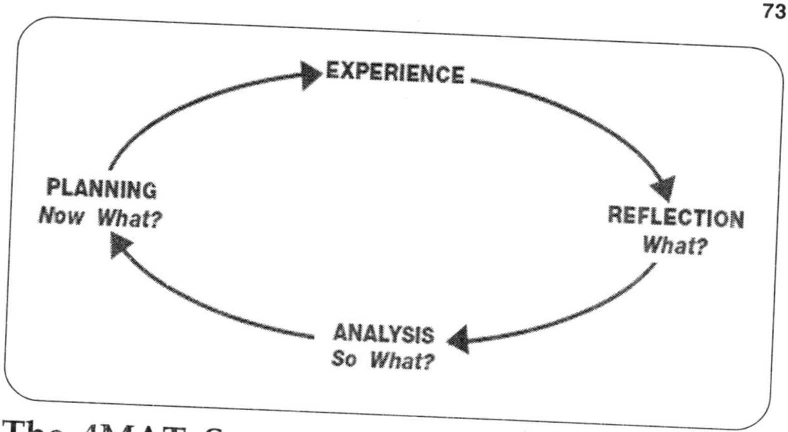

The 4MAT System

In the 1980s, educator Bernice McCarthy drew upon Kolb's work, the work of those theorists who describe left and right brain processes, and other research into learning styles to create her 4MAT System. McCarthy's theory consolidates a number of research findings into four learning styles:

Type One: The Imaginative Learners

- Perceive information concretely and process it reflectively
- Integrate experience with the self; believe in their own experiences
- Learn by listening and sharing ideas
- Excel in viewing direct experience from many perspectives
- Favorite question is: "Why?"

Type Two: The Analytic Learners

- Perceive information abstractly and process it reflectively
- Devise theories
- Often need to know that the experts think
- Value sequential thinking and need details
- Enjoy traditional classrooms
- Favorite question is: "What?"

Type Three: The Common Sense Learners

- Perceive information abstractly and process it actively
- Integrate theory and practice
- Learn by testing theories and applying common sense
- Are problem-solvers, resent being given answers
- Have a limited tolerance for fuzzy ideas; prefer to get right to the point
- Favorite question is: "How does this work?"

Type Four: The Dynamic Learners

- Perceive information concretely and process it actively
- Learn by trial and error
- Excel when flexibility is needed; are adaptable and relish change

Left and Right Brain Processes

Learners with a
left-mode processing preference

- Are systematic and analytical
- Tend to solve problems by looking at the parts

Learners with a
right-mode processing preference

- Are more intuitive
- Solve problems by looking at the whole picture

- Are risk-takers
- Enrich reality by taking what is and adding something of themselves to it
- Favorite question is: "What if?"

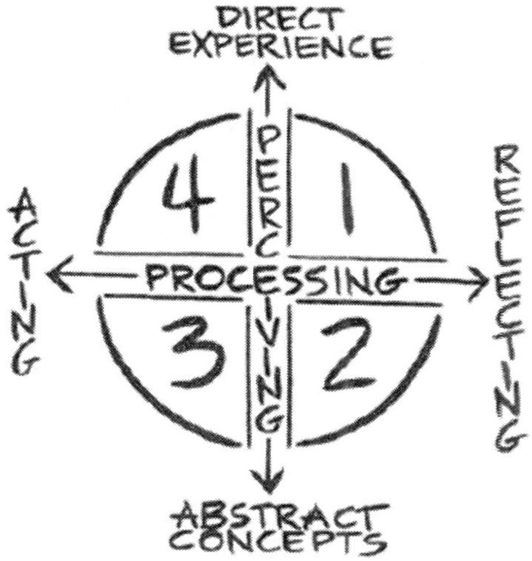

Those that are whole-brained have both gifts—they move freely between the two modes towards a fusion of analysis and intuition. Both left-mode and right-mode learners would benefit from developing the flexible use of their whole brains.

McCarthy designed her 4MAT system with this in mind. He represents her 4MAT system in the following manner:

The best lesson designs move participants through all phases of the four types of learning— allowing each kind of learner to feel comfortable part of the time, and allowing each type to strengthen skills in all the other areas.

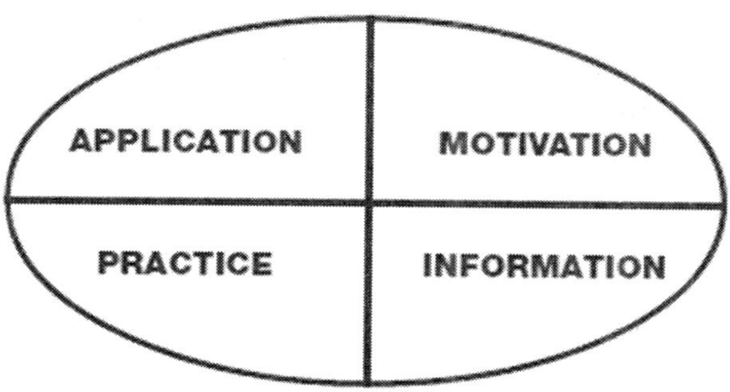

This framework for approaching lesson design has become a staple in Peace Corps' teaching and informs the Community Content-Based Instruction (CCBI) approach in particular. In the Peace Corps' version of the 4MAT System, the four quadrants are represented slightly different than in McCarthy's original text:

As you can see, this model looks a great deal like the Experiential Learning Cycle, and indeed, there are many similarities. Here are a few examples to help you to imagine 4MAT in action:

- Imagine you are a health Volunteer assigned to a prenatal clinic in Kazakhstan. You are working with your counterpart to teach new mothers how to treat diarrhea in their newborns. For the motivation stage, you could begin with a role play of a visit to the clinic with a sick newborn. You might then give a short lecture with flipchart visuals of the components of oral rehydration solution (ORS) for the information phase. The group could then practice making ORS after you have demonstrated it once. Finally, the new mothers could work in groups to apply new knowledge and "treat" a doll with ORS.
- You are a business development Volunteer. You are training local NGO representatives in fundraising skills. You could begin by having the group create a list of fundraising techniques that have been successful for them over the years (motivation). After that, you could give a short lecture on the advantages and disadvantages of fundraising approaches (information). The group could then read and discuss short case studies (practice). Finally, participants could create action plans for fundraising for their NGOs (application).

One Final Note on Learning Styles—Modalities

McCarthy also reminds us that there are three learning modalities:

- A visual learner learns by seeing and imagining.
- An auditory learner learns by listening and verbalizing.
- A kinesthetic learner learns by doing and manipulating.

All learners profit by the use of multiple learning modalities in educational programs.

Activity Planning Strategies

Now that you have a basic understanding of learning styles, the experiential learning cycle, and the 4MAT approach to lesson design, you might be thinking: "But where do I begin?" Like any successful event, the key is good and thorough planning. Begin by considering your audience, your purpose, and the resources you have on hand.

Seven Steps of Planning

Educator Jane Vella offers a useful approach when preparing for a lesson or workshop. Her *Seven Steps of Planning* provides a simple, efficient template to keep in mind when beginning to design lessons.

Who?	Who are the participants? How much do they already know about the topic? What are the age ranges, gender breakdown, cultural mix and hierarchies at work?
Why?	What is the overall goal of the learning? What do the participants want to learn? Are they attending the training voluntarily?
When?	How much time is available for the training? Are there any work or season-related time constraints? Is one time of day better than another for your participants?

Where? Where will the training be held? Indoors or outside? What equipment is available? Chairs? Tables? Flipcharts? Local materials?

What for? What are the behavioral objectives of the training? What will the participants be able to do differently after the training?

What? What specifically will participants learn? What new knowledge, skills and attitudes do you want to develop?

How? What learning activities will participants engage in to learn the content? What are all the steps of the training? How will you evaluate the training?

By using Vella's *Seven Steps* as a checklist, you can be sure that you have taken all aspects of the training into consideration as you work through your design. As you become more comfortable as a facilitator, you will undoubtedly develop your own framework for planning your lessons.

Parts of a Learning Activity

Once you've gone through the seven steps, you are ready to design the lesson/activity. Although there are as many different templates with which to plan a lesson as there are groups conducting training, the parts of a lesson are basically the same.

Warm-up: A short (5-10 minute) activity used to "break the ice" or to energize a group. Warm-ups can be used at the beginning of an activity, after breaks, after lunch and at times of low energy.

Introduction: An activity used at the beginning of a lesson that allows participants to be introduced to each other and to the facilitator(s).

Ground Rules: Also called "group norms" or "guiding principles." Ground rules help to establish a set of factors that participants agree to use while working together. They usually address the language to be used, punctuality and so on. Depending on the formality of your lesson, you may or may not negotiate the ground rules with your group.

Expectations: In this part of the lesson, participants are typically guided through an activity to express what they expect from the training. The group then reviews the agenda and the goals of the lesson to make sure everyone is in agreement.

Activities: This is the body of the lesson. What learning methods, techniques and tools will you use to communicate and explore the content of the lesson?

Evaluation: Also known as "proof of learning." An evaluation at the end of a lesson or workshop provides facilitators, participants, donors and others with feedback regarding the effectiveness of the activity or workshop design. Some approaches to activity and workshop evaluations are described on the next page.

Affirmation: Similar to an evaluation, a workshop affirmation (or reflection) is a short activity at the end of an activity to allow participants to reflect on their learning experience and provide feedback.

Be sure to design NFE experiences in partnership with your counterpart so that you learn from each other. Involving your counterpart or other HCN colleague will also help to build capacity and ensure sustainability of the program. Your colleague will also provide valuable culturally relevant information and approaches.

Writing Objectives

One useful guide for ensuring that the lesson's objectives involve as many kinds of learning as possible is to follow the "ABCs" when setting objectives.

A: Affective — what we feel; this objective involves new attitudes or feelings that have changed as a result of the activity.

B: Behavioral — what we do; this objective refers to new skills learned and practiced during the activity.

C: Cognitive — what we think; this objective involves new knowledge gained during the activity.

For example, your objectives might read:

By the end of this workshop, participants will be able to:

- describe the nutritional benefits of adding soybeans to traditional bread (cognitive);
- prepare traditional bread made with soybeans (behavioral); or
- demonstrate an understanding of the importance of eating soybean-enriched bread to their family's health (affective).

Note that each sample objective above begins with an action verb: describe, prepare and demonstrate. Additionally, to ensure that a learning experience is effective and to be able to evaluate whether people have learned, write objectives that are SMART:

S pecific,
M easurable,
A chievable,
R ealistic, and
T ime-bound.

The KSAs (Knowledge—Skills—Attitudes) at the beginning of each chapter in this manual are another description of different kinds of learning objectives, and they correspond directly to the affective, behavioral, and cognitive categories described above.

Monitoring and Evaluation

As we indicated in the Parts of a Learning Activity earlier, it is important to conduct some type of evaluation of your activity's success. Among other benefits, evaluations help you to continually improve the program, to get a sense of satisfaction for the work you are doing, and potentially, to provide evidence that could be used to justify funding or other support by the project's supporters.

Although evaluations are usually completed at the end of an activity or training, you will also want to consider some monitoring activities so you can measure your progress as you conduct the activity. You may choose to use a monitoring activity at the end of a training day, twice a day (before lunch and at the end of the day), or possibly at the end of every activity. In a highly participatory workshop, monitoring activities provide participants with an opportunity to modify the training design to better suit their needs.

It is smart to build in monitoring and evaluation while you design your activity. If you need to quantify your work, for example, you should determine the methods you will use to collect information at the beginning rather than scramble to fill information gaps at the end. In short, monitoring and evaluation activities help you measure the progress of your activity, allow you to make subtle changes if necessary, and help you to maintain timelines and group interest.

Who Wants to Know and for What Purpose?

Useful questions to consider when designing an evaluation for your learning activity or workshop are: "Who wants to know and for what purpose?" Considering these two questions may help you to decide the most appropriate approach to evaluation. Potential answers to "who wants to know?" may include the facilitators, any donors or sponsors or perhaps the participants themselves. Possible answers to "for what purpose?" may include improving subsequent activities, ascertaining follow-up training for participants, determining whether or not to fund such learning activities in the future, etc. There may be multiple answers to each of the questions, as well. For example, an evaluation of an NFE project funded by a development agency may need to serve the pragmatic purpose of renewing the funding and, at the same time, help the facilitators discover ways to improve the workshop. Therefore, it is important to ask: "who wants to know and for what purpose?" when deciding what approach to use in the evaluation of an activity or workshop.

Levels of Evaluation

In 1959, Donald Kirkpatrick developed a four-level model of evaluation. Since that time, his model has become the most widely used approach to evaluating training programs.

Level 1 Evaluation—Reactions: Just as the name implies, this simple evaluation measures participants' satisfaction with the training. Did they like it? Which activities did they like the most? Which activities would they improve? At bare minimum, educators should evaluate at this level so that they can improve their training program. Examples of this type of evaluation might include the Mood Meter.

Level 2 Evaluation—Learning: This evaluation attempts to assess to what extent the objectives have been achieved. Ideally, trainers will conduct a pre-test and a post-test to evaluate learning gains.

Level 3 Evaluation—Behavior: This level of evaluation is perhaps the best measure of an activity's effectiveness, as it seeks to discover to what extent the new knowledge, skills, or attitudes have changed the behavior of the participants. It is also, in many ways, the most difficult type of evaluation to do, as it is important to separate out any potential other reasons for this behavior change. An example of this type of evaluation might be a six-month post-training questionnaire.

Level 4 Evaluation—Results: This type of evaluation seeks to document the results that have been achieved as a result of the activity. For example, if the HIV prevalence rate in a community declines after repeated HIV/AIDS prevention training, one might conclude that the training was responsible for the decline. Again, this may be difficult to prove, as it will be necessary to ensure that nothing else was responsible for the results.

For the most part, Volunteers will probably engage in level 1 and level 2 evaluations.

Qualitative and Quantitative Evaluation

The two overarching types of data that one might collect from an evaluation (or a needs assessment, for that matter) are qualitative and quantitative. The basic distinction between them is that qualitative data refer to non-numerical information, while quantitative data refer to information that can be gathered numerically. There are advantages and disadvantages to each type of evaluation, and it is generally recommended to attempt to gather both—some numbers to allow for accurate comparison of information, and some stories or open-ended answers to capture a deeper understanding of participants' attitudes and opinions.

- Think about Tracy's training program. How might she gather quantitative information to evaluate her lessons? Qualitative information?
- What are some of the advantages and disadvantages of quantitative information? Qualitative?
- Which type of evaluation are you most comfortable with? Do you see any link between this and your preferred learning style?

Workshop Evaluations

When most people think of a workshop evaluation, they imagine a written document of one or more pages that solicits specific feedback about the activities or the overall training design. While such a written evaluation may be an important or essential part of your training, there are also a number of participatory approaches to evaluating a workshop.

Workshop Affirmations/Workshop Closing Activities

Even if you engage in one of the workshop evaluations, you may still wish to conclude your workshop or activity with an affirmation. As we mentioned earlier, an affirmation offers participants the chance to affirm the importance of the group's time together and to look ahead to the future. An affirmation or closing exercise is a short 5-15 minute activity used at the end of a learning activity or workshop. A good closing exercise fosters a sense of accomplishment by giving participants the opportunity to share their impressions of the workshop, relay appreciative messages to the group and/or reflect on what they have learned.

Create a "Spider Web" of Support

Try a "spider web" activity as a closing exercise. The "spider web" results in a visual image of the new network that has been created among the participants in the group. Direct participants to stand in a tight circle. Start off the web by making a short statement about the workshop or about the group's time together. The statement can be something positive you have noticed or learned, a new understanding or appreciation for the group or for the time that the group has spent together. After speaking and asking other participants to make a similar statement, toss a ball of string or twine to a participant across the circle, while holding on to one end of the ball of string. The participant should catch the ball of string, make a statement about the workshop and hold on to a piece of the string before tossing the ball to someone across the circle. This continues until all participants have made a statement about the training, are holding on to the string, and have tossed the ball of string to another participant.

When all participants have spoken, the final person tosses the ball of string back to you (the facilitator). If you would like, you can make some closing comments about the training. Specifically, describe the web of understanding that now connects the participants and represents the support each participant can provide for the group's well-being in the future. Visually represent this support by asking one participant to relax his or her hold on the string briefly. The web will weaken and sag, thereby visibly indicating that the web is weaker without each and every participant keeping it strong.

Note: A variation on this training has participants given a statement about the contributions of the person to whom they will pass the ball of string. This is an effective way to provide positive feedback to all members of the group.

Ideas and Applications

Now that you have read and learned about learning styles, lesson design and evaluation, it may be helpful for you to apply what you have learned. Feel free to try one, several or all of these activities.

Observe Learning Styles in your Community or Workplace

Spend a day or a week observing your host family, your community members and/or the people you work with. Ask yourself the following questions:

- How do people learn?
- Do people take notes at meetings?
- Do people ask questions when they are learning?
- What kinds of questions do they ask?
- How do children learn new games and skills?
- Can you identify a preferred learning style in the community?
- Do school lessons incorporate different learning styles?
- Which stage of the 4MAT do you think would be most unfamiliar to community members?
- How might your observations of learning styles affect your approach to teaching and training?

Facilitate a "Learning Styles Awareness" Activity

Use the "Learning to Sail" activity with a group of trainees, trainers, counterparts, or friends to help build awareness of each person's different learning style.

Determine Attitudes and Assumptions about Learning and Education.

Interview community members (parents, local leaders, teachers, principals, business people, children). Some questions you might ask include:

- Did you enjoy school? What was your favorite subject? What was your favorite type of lesson?
- Do you think people learn differently?
- Why is learning important? What is the value of learning and education? How much education is enough?
- What do you think are the characteristics of a good student? A good teacher?
- Should students ask questions of their teachers? Why? Why not?

Practice Using Processing Questions

One way of helping learners move through the four learning stages is by asking them questions. Think back on what you read about the work of Kolb and McCarthy on learning styles. Then look at the list of questions below. Which questions would be most appropriate for the reflection stage? Which ones are good for the generalization stage? The application stage?

- What are the consequences of doing/not doing this?
- Can someone describe what we just did?
- In what ways does this change your understanding of the situation?
- What happened next?
- Does this remind you of anything? What can it help explain?
- What surprised you? Puzzled you?

- How might you improve this situation?
- What were the steps involved?
- What are some of the major themes at work here?
- What struck you as particularly important or significant?
- What did you learn from this experience?
- How did you feel about what happened?
- How might you apply this to your own situation?
- How can you account for what happened?
- What lessons can be learned from this?
- How might it have been different?
- How does this experience relate to other experiences?
- What does this suggest to you about yourself or your group?

Use Tools to Identify Learning Styles

With your new understanding of learning styles, can you devise a method to help learners discover their own learning styles? Whether it is a written questionnaire, a participatory activity or something else, what method would you suggest for guiding participants to an understanding of their own learning styles?

If you have access to the Internet, type "learning styles inventory" into any major search engine and choose from a variety of free online resources that offer online questionnaires to determine your own learning style. Do this for yourself, or, if you have access to a computer lab, lead a group through a learning styles discovery activity.

See the "Web Resources" at the end of the chapter for some suggested learning styles inventories offered online free of charge.

Reflect

- Why is an understanding of learning styles important when designing a learning activity?
- What makes the experiential learning cycle particularly powerful as an NFE approach?
- Why is evaluation a crucial component in NFE lesson design?

Key Resources

References:

Kirkpatrick, Donald L. *Evaluating Training Programs: The Four Levels*. San Francisco: Berrett- Koehler Publications, 1998.

In this newest edition of his groundbreaking 1959 text, Kirkpatrick describes his four-level approach to evaluating learning programs—evaluating reaction, learning, behavior, and results. "The Kirkpatrick Model" is probably the most-used approach for evaluating training programs.

Kolb, David A. *Experiential Learning: Experience as the Source of Learning and Development*. New Jersey: Prentice Hall TPR, 1983.

This text provides the theoretical and practical underpinnings of Kolb's learning styles theory, and introduces the experiential learning cycle. The book also includes Kolb's Learning Styles Inventory.

McCarthy, Bernice. *The 4MAT System: Teaching to Learning Styles with Right/Left Mode Techniques*. Barrington, IL: EXCEL, Inc., 1987. [ICE No. ED187]

McCarthy combines Kolb's theories with research on left- and right-mode processing preference to create her 4MAT system. This text provides a concise and clear description of McCarthy's four learning styles and suggests specific approaches for using the 4MAT system to create powerful lesson plans.

Roles of the Volunteer in Development: Toolkits for Building Capacity. Washington, DC: Peace Corps, 2002.

This text provides a comprehensive look at the place of the Volunteer in the development process. Detailing the Volunteer's roles as learner, change agent, co-trainer, co-facilitator, project co-planner, and mentor, RVID provides countless theories, case studies, activities and approaches to help Volunteers and their communities get the most of out their two years of service.

Vella, Jane. Learning to Teach: *Training of Trainers for Community and Institutional Development*. Westport, CT: Save the Children, 1989.

Vella's useful text provides 25 sample lesson plans for training trainers in adult learning, Freirian approaches, and facilitation skills. The manual also includes suggested warm-up activities and Vella's "seven steps of planning."

Additional Resources:

Community Content-Based Instruction Manual. Washington, DC: Peace Corps, 2002.

The CCBI Manual describes possibilities for incorporating culturally appropriate, real-life examples into an existing curriculum so that learning activities are more relevant to students' lives. The text draws on McCarthy's 4MAT system to suggest a powerful approach for working with students in the formal education system. A number of sample lesson plans are also provided.

Eitington, Julius E. *The Winning Trainer: Winning Ways to Involve People in Learning*. Boston: Butterworth Heinemann, 2002.

Eitington's text offers a comprehensive guide for the new trainer. The book describes hundreds of training methods and suggestions, and includes various handouts for use in learning situations. Additional topics include preparation of the learning environment and evaluation strategies.

Hope, Anne, and Sally Timmel. *Training for Transformation: A Handbook for Community Workers, Books I-IV*. London: Intermediate Technology Publications, 1999.

Written for practitioners in community development and transformative education, the Training for Transformation series suggests a powerful, wholly participatory approach to working with local people. The first book details the theories of Paulo Freire and suggests methods for developing critical awareness. The second text focuses on the skills necessary for participatory education and suggests methods for actively involving the group. Book three deals with social analysis and provides tools for long-term planning and building solidarity. The final text in the series applies the approach to current topics of racism, environmental degradation, and women's issues.

McCarthy, Bernice. *About Teaching: 4Mat in the Classroom*. Wauconda, IL: About Learning, Inc., 2000.

For more information about McCarthy's 4MAT System of learning and teaching, refer to this updated and revised version. As in the earlier edition, McCarthy combines Kolb's theories with research on left- and right-mode processing preference to create her 4MAT system. This updated text provides a description of McCarthy's four learning styles and suggests specific approaches for using the 4MAT system to create powerful lesson plans.

Technology of Participation: Group Facilitation Methods: Effective Methods for Participation. Phoenix, AZ: Institute for Cultural Affairs, 1991, 1994, 1996, 2000.

This manual details participatory approaches to action planning and consensus building. The text also suggests a "focused conversation" method of processing learning activities, including a number of powerful questions to use with the experiential learning cycle.

VIPP: Visualisation in Participatory Programmes. Bangladesh: UNICEF, 1993.

This classic text details a people-centered approach to planning, training, and group consensus building. At the core of the VIPP methodology is the use of multi-colored cards, highly visual learning aids, and strong facilitation based on a commitment to the principles of adult learning. The text offers specific exercises for participatory group work, including games, exercises, debates, card sorting, and evaluation ideas.

Vella, Jane. *How Do They Know They Know?* San Francisco: Jossey-Bass, 1997.

In this fascinating text, Vella applies the principles of non-formal education to evaluation. Through theory and practical examples, Vella suggests an approach for using participation, dialogue, and adult learning theory to evaluate learning programs.

Working with Youth: Approaches for Volunteers. Washington, DC: Peace Corps, 2002.

This informative guide to working with youth includes a comprehensive section on participatory assessment. Techniques include Venn diagrams, informal interviews, group interviews, community mapping, and tips for compiling information. The text also includes a lesson on participatory planning.

Chapter – 4

CREATING AN EFFECTIVE LEARNING ENVIRONMENT

NFE In Action: Considering the Learning Environment

RUTH

Ruth finishes sweeping, grabs her schoolbooks and runs towards the school. She is late again, and she knows the teacher will be angry with her and remind her that if she doesn't pass her exams, she'll never make it to secondary school. Even though she wakes up early every morning, she just has so much to do—getting the water, helping her mother get bathwater and breakfast ready—there just isn't enough time for it all. When she reaches the schoolyard, classes have already begun. She slips into her classroom, conscious of the scowl on her teacher's face. She has arrived there too late to get one of the desks, so she crowds into the back of the room

	KNOWLEDGE	SKILLS	ATTITUDES
Knowledge, skills, and attitudes needed to create an effective learning environment	• Characteristics of an effective learning environment • Important physical aspects conducive to learning • Climate-setting techniques • Gender and cross-cultural issues that impact learning • Aspects of group management	• Arrangement of space and materials • Writing and drawing skills • Ability to set a climate and facilitate learning • Language skills and cross-cultural communication skills • Ability to assess group dynamics • Ability to balance individual learner and group needs	• Confidence • Self-awareness • Genuine interest in participants and the topic • Commitment to participatory learnings • Flexibility
Your strengths			
Your plans to learn more			

with some other latecomers, sitting on the floor and arranging her books around her. The room is hot and cramped, and it is so difficult to hear the teacher from the back! Ruth strains to see the chalkboard and begins to work on the lesson... Think about Ruth's situation for a moment. Even if her teacher designs lessons for every learning style, even if the sessions are participatory and the content is relevant, would you describe Ruth's learning experience as effective? What are some of the issues at work in Ruth's story? A successful educator must be able to focus on the lesson design elements that we discussed in Chapter 3, while simultaneously considering all of the factors necessary to create an effective learning environment. Good teachers have always been conscious of the effect of arrangement, spatial issues, temperature, and other external factors on learning. In the 1980s, Malcolm Knowles elaborated on the importance of environment in his adult learning theory and since that time, a rich field of research has explored the relationship of the environment to effective learning. Too often, the focus on learning environment is limited to room arrangement, but effective educators must take into consideration all of the factors that the physical and emotional surroundings bring to the day's learning.

Consider Ruth's learning environment from earlier in the chapter.

- What physical surroundings may have had an impact on her learning?
- Were any psychological or emotional conditions at work in her story?
- What social or cultural influences may have had an impact on her learning?
- How much of these factors are under your control as a teacher or facilitator?

Physical Environment

How can you create a physical environment that supports and enhances learning? There are several factors to consider when choosing or utilizing a space for effective learning.

- **Size:** How many participants or students are you expecting? Will the area be large enough? Is there another area that might better fit the group? If you have no other room choices, how might you best maximize the space in the area? Can you move outside? Are there pieces of furniture that you might remove or adjust to make the room more comfortable? Remember to consider crosscultural issues of space when answering these questions, as different cultures have different comfort zones in terms of personal space.

- **Arrangement:** Consider the activities you have planned. What is the best arrangement for those activities? A circle of chairs? A semi-circle? Should part of the room be free of furniture to allow space to move, or is a space available for interactive activities outside? Does the arrangement you have chosen convey any implicit messages about hierarchy or authority? (For example, if you see a teacher standing behind a podium, with students in linear rows, what messages of authority and hierarchy might be implied? How about a circle of chairs, with the facilitator sitting in the circle?)

Temperature: Is the room too hot? Too cold? Is this something that you can control?

- **Access:** Are signs clearly visible to direct participants to the appropriate room? Does the building allow access for people of differing physical abilities? Are restrooms available nearby? Are they comfortable?
- **Cleanliness:** Is the room clean? Is the furniture in good condition?
- **Visuals:** Can participants clearly see you? Can they clearly see each other? Are any views blocked by columns, furniture, glare, other participants? Is there adequate lighting? If you are using a flipchart, chalkboard, or audiovisual equipment, be sure to preview these before the sessions. Write something on the flipchart or chalkboard, or turn on the television, overhead projector, or computer, then look at these visuals from different angles and distances. Is your handwriting legible? Can everyone see clearly? Are the markers you're using hard to see?
- **Hearing and Sounds:** Are you projecting your voice loudly enough so that participants hear you? Are there any noises that might distract the participants?
- **Decoration:** Are there ways to decorate the training space to make it more appealing and more informative? Are there any posters, maps or other wall hangings that would add to the learning experience? Do you have texts, handouts or other resources that might be left in the back of the room on a resource table? Be sure to consider the literacy levels and the language of your participants when deciding on posters and written resources. Also, be aware of any taboos around what images might be depicted on such posters and texts. As the workshop or classroom experience progresses, you may find that the most inspiring "decorations" will be the output from the sessions— flipcharts from small group work, lists of ground rules, expectations, objectives, and so forth. But in the beginning, feel free to make the space feel comfortable, attractive, and representative of the topic you will be addressing in the learning experience.

Using "Toys" in the Adult Learning Environment

One way to use the physical environment to tap in to the energy of the "right brain processes" that we discussed in Chapter 3 is to scatter "toys" on participants' tables or workspaces. These "toys" can be almost anything—squishy balls, clay, magnets, tiny plastic gadgets, something funny from the market—anything that participants can quietly and thoughtlessly play with while they are working on a project or listening to a lecture. By tapping into the participants' desire for "play" and creativity, you engage their right brain/kinesthetic mode of learning. Although it seems like a distraction, you are actually achieving broader levels of concentration. This tactic is especially useful when participants will be working together in groups on a difficult topic, or when energy seems to be low. Although you and your co-facilitators will probably have to attend to all of the issues around physical environment in the beginning of the workshop, session, or semester, be sure to involve participants in these decisions as your work together progresses. You might do this by:

- **Conducting a quick space needs assessment:** Ask participants how comfortable they are with the room, temperature, arrangement and so forth at the beginning and at various points throughout the sessions. You might wish to do this verbally and on a quick written form, the latter to capture the needs of quieter participants.

- **Inviting participants to get comfortable:** Give permission for participants to make changes to the learning environment or to their own positions so that they remain comfortable, satisfied, and engaged in the learning process.

- **Create participant committees:** Empower a participant group to take charge of some of these issues—decorations, for example, or a resource table.

Climate Setting

Once you have worked out the session design and created a comfortable physical space, you'll want to give some thought to the type of climate or atmosphere you will create in the learning environment. The first day of the group's work together is probably the most important opportunity to set the tone for the entire learning experience. Every learner—whether adult or youth—brings certain anxieties and expectations to a new learning situation. It is up to you and the rest of the facilitation team to make participants comfortable and to project an atmosphere that will be conducive to learning. The answers to the following three key questions should be clear by the end of the first day.

- **Who are we?** Through introductions, a discussion of expectations and icebreakers, participants should be given an opportunity to bring their own personalities, interests and backgrounds into the group. Depending on the situation, this may also be the time to clarify how the group will work together, perhaps through the creation of group norms or ground rules.
- **Who is the facilitator?** Participants want to learn a bit about you in this first session, so that they may begin to feel comfortable and secure in their relationship with you. Often, training manuals refer to the importance of establishing credibility, however, it is probably equally (or more) important for the NFE practitioner to make explicit his or her role as a learner in the process. This is especially true when working with adults, as you will want to make it clear that your time together will represent a sharing of everyone's experiences.
- **What is the purpose?** Finally, the first day should clarify the purpose of your time together. Discuss and post the objectives and agenda so the day's schedule is clear to all. You may want to describe any needs assessments that

may have helped to shape the agenda, and briefly outline the proposed content of the learning experience.

Deciding what tone to set will depend on several factors, including your own personality, the audience, the cultural norms, and the topic of the learning experience. For example, if the topic of your learning experience is caring for people living with HIV/AIDS, a tone of serious hopefulness is probably more appropriate than the cheerful excitement you might project if the session were about building a community center.

INCLUSION: When a group forms, people must interact and get attention so that they feel included. This takes time. People feel included when they hear their names mentioned, when they respond to open questions, and when they perform a task with a small group. If a person does not experience inclusion, he or she may not fully participate in later learning activities. When a new person joins the group late, that person has the same need for inclusion. In fact, there is a new group when a newcomer arrives. So the process of inclusion must take place all over again.

Creating Community in a Learning Environment

A crucial aspect of climate setting is creating a feeling of community among participants in a learning environment. Take a look at the following examples and try to identify the potentially uncomfortable issues involved.

- A woman is encouraged to join a small, all-male group to discuss issues of gender.
- Three junior teachers are asked to perform a role play with their district's education supervisor.

- During the opening speech, a group of government officials is told that its performance on the post test at the end of the workshop will be a big factor when determining promotions.
- A Volunteer rapidly asks a difficult question in English to a villager.
- At a community meeting, the facilitator from an international NGO uses jokes and irony to lighten the mood after an intense discussion of the community's needs.

Participants are in a better position to learn and share their experiences when they feel comfortable and confident in their learning environment. To create a safe space, it is important to truly understand the participant group with which you are working. Remember to assess your community carefully, taking your time to observe, cultivate relationships with members of the community, and include community members in your activity-planning processes. Discuss the issues of gender, culture, hierarchy, language, and typical ways of learning in the host community or culture. Keep in mind that while humor can be useful in creating a positive atmosphere; take care to respect cultural norms. You may want to begin on safer ground, and then challenge the group little by little as the group becomes closer and more comfortable with each other, with you, and with the content.

Considering Gender and Culture in the Learning Environment

Think back to the story about Ruth earlier in this chapter. Can you identify any factors that inhibited Ruth's learning experience as a direct result of her gender?

- Suppose the many tasks Ruth needs to complete each morning before she can leave for school are tasks usually assigned to the girls in the family. What implications does this have for Ruth's schooling?

- If the girls in the classroom are late each day because of these chores and there aren't enough seats for all of the students, who do you think is always sitting on the floor in the back of the room? Who, then, is sitting at the desks in the front? What implications does this have for the learning experiences of the girls? Of the boys?
- How do you think the teacher's gender might affect the learning environment? How might it affect the teacher's interaction with boys? With girls?
- What can you do as an educator to promote a positive learning experience for both the girls and the boys in a situation like this one?

In every area, there are gender issues, cultural issues, and issues of race, religion, and class that may impact the learning experience. Although there are no definitive answers for every such situation, it is important for you to:

- Educate yourself about the issues of gender, culture, class, religion, and race that may have an impact on the learning experience.
- Consult with HCN counterparts and friends regarding culturally appropriate solutions to some of these situations.
- Devise creative approaches to lessen the impact of these issues on the learning experience. For example, in Ruth's situation, you might have a seating chart that changes weekly, so that each student gets a turn at a desk in the front of the classroom. Or you might try to rearrange the room, perhaps using only small chairs, so that all students can see clearly.
- Discuss these situations and make them a part of the learning process. Subtly and respectfully examining issues of hierarchy is a fundamental component of NFE since power and status are often less obvious in nonformal settings than in formal settings where these roles are usually more clear. Conducting sessions or having discussions around the

impact of gender, multiculturalism, religion, and class may offer opportunities to enhance the learning environment and may even lead to lasting change.

It is important not to assume that the impact of gender on education applies only to girls. In Lesotho, for example, some boys have more difficulty gaining access to education. Boys work as shepherds when they are very young and may only be sent to school years later, at which time they are placed into classrooms with girls half their age. In Mongolia, because of the shepherding duties, boys are often pulled out of school. In Jamaica, girls are given preference— if only some children can go to school, then the girls go. What impact might these cultural differences have on the boys? On the young girls they share a classroom with? On the learning experience?

The Art of Facilitation

Facilitation is an art and a craft. It is a craft in that the facilitator must know and follow the rules, learn how to pose the right question at the right moment and write clearly. It is also an art that requires experience and intuition since the facilitator must create a drama that allows the group to give all of its potential to the process. The facilitator must be able to creatively get the group out of situations of conflict and to respond to the requirements of the group at any moment by adopting a new technique or by accepting an idea coming from the group.

Once the design is finished, the physical environment established, and your plan for climate setting and activities is in place, it is show time! Most of the "art" of facilitation comes from experience—the more you work with groups, the more likely you will be comfortable responding to the myriad situations that will come up in any meeting, gathering, workshop, or classroom. Here are a few basic facilitation guidelines to make your first few experiences most effective:

Planning

- Incorporate and use a variety of activities. As we learned in Chapter 3, participants have different learning styles. Varying the pace and type of activities will help to stimulate learning. You may wish to use the experiential learning cycle, 4MAT, or another of the theories discussed in Chapter 3 to guide you in choosing the appropriate activities for all learning styles. In the next chapter, we will look at specific techniques and methods you can use to keep participants involved and motivated.
- Pay attention to pace and timing. Will you be presenting completely new information to the group? If so, you may wish to allow more time for discussion and reflection so that the learners can digest the new material. Are you working with children or adults? Children tend to need more variety and frequent changes of pace, whereas adults can focus for greater lengths of time.
- Come prepared with necessary supplies.
- Check your handouts, flipcharts and other visual aids for accuracy and legibility. If your handwriting is not good, consider enlisting someone to help you to create visuals.
- Use a pencil to make notes to yourself on prepared flipcharts – the participants won't be able to see them. Plan how you will write on flipcharts or the blackboard in advance when you can, so you won't run out of space and the flow is logical.
- Practice the techniques you will use beforehand so you don't get too nervous or lose your train of thought. Visualize the entire session or meeting the night before—imagining how you will arrange the room, what you will say, how you will make transitions between activities, etc. Jot short notes on a card to briefly refer to during the session.

Implementing

- Be positive and confident. Smile.
- Communicate enthusiasm for the meeting, the topic and the people involved.
- Express genuine interest in each individual's contribution to the discussion.
- Speak loudly and clearly enough for everyone to hear easily, and enunciate words—especially if you, or the participants, are struggling with a second language.
- Use open questions, rather than closed questions. Open questions invite discussion and critical thinking, while closed questions evoke short answers. For example, the open-ended question: "How might we encourage Ruth to participate in class better?" invites a thoughtful response. The closed question: "Do you think Ruth is able to participate in the class?" may limit the learner to a one word answer.

- Encourage discussion among group members instead of between participants and yourself. You can do this by redirecting questions to the entire group, perhaps by saying: "What do you think of Mr. Gomez's suggestion?"
- Use small group discussions to foster greater communication and participation. You can form small groups in many different ways.
- Ask participants to count off around the room. If you want four groups, they should count to four as you go around the

room. Then, all the "ones" form a group, all the "twos" and so forth.

- Ask people to self-select into groups with people they don't know.
- Write the name of different animals, colors or foods on cards around the room, and tell participants to go to the one they like the most. If you are working on specific topics, you might write down the different topic choices instead, so that participants can self-select groups according to the topic that resonates for them.
- Try to keep the meeting or session from drifting too far off topic. It takes some practice to balance facilitator control with group participation. Use your tone of voice, your energy or "presence" and your interested silence to keep the group focused.
- Let participants know when you have learned something new from them.
- Write legibly in dark colors. It helps to alternate between two colors when writing on a flipchart or chalkboard.

Follow-up

- Set aside some reflection time immediately after a session or workshop to reflect on your and your learners' experiences. Consider what worked well and what could be improved in the future. What parts of the session went really well? Were there times or situations where you really had to stretch as a facilitator? What did you learn about yourself? About the group? How can you build on that learning in the future?
- Immediately after the session, add your reflections on, and reactions to, the session to the bottom of your notes so they are there for you the next time you do that session.
- Compile any notes, feedback, evaluation results or action plans and distribute them to the participants as appropriate.

- If you plan to facilitate a similar session in the future, take stock of your supplies and resources. Do you need to revise any materials? Create new ones? Order or create more supplies?

Cross-cultural Group Facilitation

Facilitating a group in a culture different from your own is tricky, since how people behave may have entirely different meanings than you expect. In the U.S., if group members are silent, it could be assumed they are shy, that they don't have any ideas on the subject, or that they are intimidated by other group members (including the facilitator). But in some cultures, the highest-status individuals may be the quietest, showing their wisdom and respect for others by their ability to reflect and hold back the first ideas that come to mind.

Setting an agenda, giving feedback, dealing with disruptions, keeping the group on task and gaining consensus are all culturally based behaviors. Expecting groups in your host country to act like Americans can be frustrating and counterproductive. Use your crosscultural skills and your ability to observe and ask discreet questions to understand group behavior in your host country before trying to facilitate groups in your work as a Volunteer. Look for some of the following:

- What formalities are observed? Who opens and closes the meeting, and how is this typically accomplished?
- Where do people of different status sit?
- How are topics introduced? By going straight to the point? Indirectly?
- Which topics are introduced first? (In some cultures, the most important topics are saved until last.)
- What irrelevant topics are introduced? Are they really irrelevant? How do people get permission—or find an opening—to speak?
- How long does it typically take the group to decide on something? What is the process for coming to a decision? (Look for differences here between the "All in favor say 'aye'" approach and a lengthy discussion process in which everyone has a chance to air his or her views but complete consensus is expected in the end.) How do members of the group express their dissatisfaction with one another? What kinds of decisions are made outside the meeting? Where and how are they made? By whom?

Encouraging Healthy Group Dynamics

As we noted earlier, one of the most challenging yet rewarding aspects of facilitating is empowering participants to take charge of their own learning. Effective facilitators capitalize on teachable moments and create opportunities for learners to participate. Encouraging, recognizing and then allowing those moments to happen is largely a function of understanding and managing group dynamics. Below are some tips for fostering healthy group dynamics.

- **Encourage open discussion:** Let the participants know they don't have to agree—either with each other or with you. Be clear that they are free to come to their own conclusions, learn what they want to learn, and reject what they don't agree with. At the same time, try to keep the group on track by letting them know when it is time to move on.

- **Break off lengthy discussions kindly:** Interesting discussions must sometimes be cut short in order to respect time constraints or cover other important topics. If several people have indicated that they still have something to say, you might say something like: "Okay, first Georgi, then Lydia, then Elena, and then we'll have to move on because we're running out of time." This is both more respectful and more effective than just trying to end the discussion abruptly.

- **Integrate the big talkers, encourage the silent types:** Often a group will have one or two highly vocal participants who tend to dominate the discussion as well as a few who seem interested but keep their ideas to themselves. You can balance the group a bit better by trying some of the following:
  - Don't force the quiet ones to talk by calling on them. People have different learning styles. Some prefer to quietly reflect rather than speak publicly what first comes to mind. Try to balance the desire for full participation with the learning styles of various participants.

- Frequently change the makeup of small groups. This way, quieter people will eventually meet up with other quiet types and be able to speak up, while the talkers will meet and be challenged by talkers like themselves.
- In a large group discussion, after asking for ideas on some topic, ask participants to jot down one or two ideas before anyone speaks, then go around the room and ask each person to read one idea.
- Look for body language. People who are ready with ideas often sit forward, or meet your eyes, or shift in their seats while another person is speaking.

  If a participant really begins to dominate the discussion, talk to that person after the session and enlist their help in encouraging others to speak up.
- Remember that there may be a cultural reason for lack of participation, or it may be the result of gender roles. If a situation seems particularly unclear to you, talk with an HCN co-facilitator about it, or you might want to raise the question in the group during a reflection or evaluation period.

When the whole group is silent: When people feel hesitant about speaking up, or when it is hot or people are tired, you may have difficulty getting discussion started. If you ask a question and no one answers it, wait—count to five very slowly to yourself without betraying any anxiety or irritation. Be comfortable with the silence. If no one answers, smile, rephrase the question and wait again. If discussion continues to be slow, consider using "buzz groups," in which participants discuss the question with a partner for a few minutes. Then go around the room, asking several pairs what they came up with—the whole group may be surprised at the number of good ideas that emerge. Or, have people individually write down points and then ask if anyone wants to share. If no one volunteers, move on.

Ideas and Applications

Now that you have read about learning environments, it may be helpful for you to apply what you have learned. Feel free to try one, several or all of these activities.

Brainstorm Components of a Powerful Learning Experience

With a member of your training group or a friend at your site, exchange stories about powerful learning experiences from your past—a workshop, classroom session, or meeting that you consider to have had the most effective learning environment. Tell a story about this learning experience, and include answers to some of the following questions. What was the session like?

- What made it such a positive experience? Describe the physical space.
- What was the room arrangement like?
- How did the facilitator/teacher set the climate?
- How did the facilitator ensure that the different learning styles of participants were met?
- How did participants interact?
- What were the factors of success for these sessions?
- How might you incorporate these factors into the learning experiences you facilitate?

Assess a Learning Environment

Whether at pre-service training, in-service training, or at your site, consider conducting an assessment of the learning environment at the next workshop you attend. Use the questions listed earlier in this chapter under "Physical Environment" and "Climate Setting" to assess the physical space, arrangement, visuals, decorations, and so on.

Take a Survey of Visual Techniques

Conduct a survey of the visual techniques used in your community. Remember that communities will vary in their levels of "visual literacy." If you are working with a community that relies on verbal instructions, pictures and images used as visual aids could be confusing or misleading. The following example used in Helping Health Workers Learn illustrates the importance of considering visual literacy:

In a workshop designed to help prevent the spread of malaria, a rural health worker uses a larger than life photo of a mosquito known to carry malaria. The participants in the workshop look at the large beast and are relieved—they certainly have no large flying creatures like that to worry about in their community! If the health worker had also shown a life-sized photo or (even better) a real-live specimen, the appropriate message may have been relayed.

As you conduct your visual survey, consider the following questions to help you assess how and when your community uses visuals to convey information.

- Are there posters or billboards?
- If so, what do the posters and billboards look like?
- Are there visible educational materials?
- Are there prominent colors and/or styles?
- How much writing is used?
- Are materials available for less literate audiences?
- How might you incorporate these features in your own visuals?
- Are there any cultural taboos concerning what can be pictured in public?

Create a Facilitation Checklist

Using your new knowledge about learning styles theory, creating an effective learning environment and facilitating techniques, consider creating a checklist for your own use in designing training sessions. As you continue to work through this book and as you facilitate learning experiences, you can add to and modify the checklist to make it a useful tool in your continued work in NFE. Below is a sample checklist to get you started.

- Participants meet each other
- All learners have a way to participate
- Visual aids (blackboards, posters, flipcharts, handouts) are legible

Reflect

- Why are physical environment and climate so important to the creation of an effective learning environment?
- Just as there are different learning styles, there are different facilitation styles. Consider your own learning style. How do you think it might impact your approach as a facilitator?

- Sometimes, methods of learning in the host culture might directly contradict some of the tenets of nonformal education. For example, a strict hierarchy among participants may contradict with the desire for a non-hierarchical, participatory environment. How can you as a Volunteer help participants deal with this contradiction in their work and daily life? How can you simultaneously show your respect for the culture while also "pushing the envelope" using NFE approaches?
- Often, Volunteers have little choice in the physical size of their learning environments. Education Volunteers may be given a particular classroom, and Volunteers in other sectors may only have a small room in their office, health center or community center for meetings or sessions. How might you use your facilitation skills to overcome difficulties in the physical environment like overcrowding, too few desks and so on?

Key Resources

References:

Vella, Jane. *Learning to Teach: Training of Trainers for Community and Institutional Development*. Westport, CT: Save the Children, 1989.

Vella's useful text provides 25 sample session plans for training trainers in adult learning, Freirian approaches, and facilitation skills. The manual also includes suggested warm-up activities and Vella's "seven steps of planning."

VIPP: Visualisation in Participatory Programmes. Bangladesh: UNICEF, 1993. This classic text details a people-centered approach to planning, training, and group consensus building. At the core of the VIPP methodology is the use of multi-colored cards, highly visual learning aids, and strong facilitation based on a commitment to the principles of adult learning. The text offers specific exercises for participatory group work, including games, exercises, debates, card sorting, and evaluation ideas. The book also suggests ways to structure the learning environment.

Werner, David and Bill Bower. *Helping Health Workers Learn: A Book of Methods, Aids, and Ideas for Instructors at the Village Level.* Palo Alto, CA: The Hesperian Foundation, 1982.

Although the title suggests that this book is for health workers at the village level, the messages, methods, teaching techniques, and approaches can be adapted to any learning situation. Werner and Bower effectively describe Freirian participatory approaches to education and provide a wealth of examples and strategies for using these theories in learning situations.

Additional Resource

Eitington, Julius E. *The Winning Trainer: Winning Ways to Involve People in Learning.* Boston: Butterworth Heinemann, MA, 2002.

Eitington's text offers a comprehensive guide for the new trainer. The book describes hundreds of training methods and suggestions, and includes various handouts for use in learning situations. Additional topics include preparation of the learning environment and evaluation strategies.

INDEX